Critical Inv

General Editor: John Sch

University of Lancaster

PUBLISHED
Heidegger's Bicycle
Interfering with Victorian Texts
Roger Ebbatson

The English Question; or, Academic Freedoms
Thomas Docherty

The Prodigal Sign
Kevin Mills

GIVEN: 1° Art 2° Crime
Modernity, Murder and Mass Culture
Jean-Michel Rabaté

Someone Called Derrida
An Oxford Mystery
John Schad

FORTHCOMING
The Medium is the Maker
Browning, Freud, Derrida
J. Hillis Miller

In Search of Vinteuil
Music Writing and the Literary Act of Creation
James Holden

Rapture
Literature, Secrecy, Addiction
David Punter

The Habits of Distraction
Michael Wood

John Schad is Professor of Modern Literature at Lancaster University. He is the author of *The Reader in Dickensian Mirrors*, *Victorians in Theory*, *Arthur Hugh Clough*, and *Queer Fish: Christian Unreason from Darwin to Joyce* – this last published by Sussex Academic Press. He is also the editor of *Dickens Refigured*, *Thomas Hardy's A Laodicean*, *Writing the Bodies of Christ* and co-editor of *life.after.theory*.

For Caris and Vic –

elder sister, elder brother

The
Prodigal Sign

A PARABLE OF CRITICISM

KEVIN MILLS

sussex
ACADEMIC
PRESS

BRIGHTON • PORTLAND

The right of Kevin Mills to be identified as Author of this work has been asserted in accordance with the Copyright, Designs and Patents Act 1988.

2 4 6 8 10 9 7 5 3

First published 2009 in Great Britain by
SUSSEX ACADEMIC PRESS
PO Box 139
Eastbourne BN24 9BP

and in the United States of America by
SUSSEX ACADEMIC PRESS
920 NE 58th Ave   Suite 300
Portland, Oregon 97213-3786

British Library Cataloguing in Publication Data
A CIP catalogue record for this book is available from the British Library.

Library of Congress Cataloging-in-Publication Data
Mills, Kevin.
The prodigal sign : a parable of criticism / Kevin Mills.
p. cm. — (Critical inventions)
Includes bibliographical references and index.
ISBN 978-1-84519-154-2 (h/b : alk. paper) — ISBN 978-1-84519-155-9
(p/b : alk. paper)
1. Criticism. 2. Religion and literature. 3. Parables—History and criticism. 4. Prodigal son (Parable) in literature. I. Title.
PN98.R44M55 2009
801'.95—dc22

2008029920

Mixed Sources
Product group from well-managed forests and other controlled sources
www.fsc.org Cert no. SGS-COC-2482
© 1996 Forest Stewardship Council
FSC

Typeset and designed by SAP, Brighton & Eastbourne
Printed by TJ International, Padstow, Cornwall
This book is printed on acid-free paper.

Contents

Series Editor's Preface

My friend, Kevin Mills, has run away, run away with a huge pile of books. Mind you, he has also run way *from* a pile of books, the same books – for what we have here is the critic as prodigal, the critic who sees in the Parable of the Prodigal Son a parable of criticism. In this book, my friend runs with the prodigal son in every sense. 'Escape,' he cries over his shoulder, 'is on the agenda. Indeed, escape *is* the agenda.' And so Prodigal Mills has kicked up his boot-heels and is off, legging it from a host of 'fathers, precursors, histories, influences, . . . [and] institutions' – in particular, the strange institution of literary criticism. Prodigal Mills has heard rumours of the far country they call 'creative' and has gone off to squander his academic inheritance in riotous writing – here we have not just escape but escapade.

This is reckless. It may even be suicidal if dear old Matthew Arnold is to be believed: 'Creative activity,' he famously sighed, 'is the promised land towards which criticism can only beckon. That promised land will not be ours to enter, and we shall die in the wilderness.' Prodigal Mills knows this, or at least knows that all prodigals will, at some point, sit in a wilderness, feeding the swine and envying the husks that they eat. But my friend is not so sure that we shall die in the wilderness; for he knows that it is only there that we ever have the time or need to notice such as the pigs and the husks – the remnants of life, the overlooked and forgotten.

And Prodigal Mills, it turns out, has both the time and need to notice, within the parable itself, some forgotten servants and an invisible mother. Indeed, he also gets round to noticing the forgotten and invisible person of the critic himself – it is when feeding the swine that the prodigal, we are told, 'comes to himself.' And Prodigal Mills does indeed come to himself, to the subject of himself – 'the self that not only reads and thinks but also laughs, drinks tea, and visits the bathroom.'

This self is, though, hard to find, hard to gather up; for, as my friend declares, 'I was wrecked on the way to language.' It seems that, as some comedian might say, a funny thing happened to him on the way. Or rather, several funny things – among them: Welshness, fatherhood, unemployment, literary theory, the lyrics of Bob Dylan and, above all, religion. 'The Bible,' confesses our prodigal, 'captured me in my childhood and from that I can't escape.' His mother, not-so invisible, read to him the story of the prodigal son before he could ever read it for himself.

Christianity, it seems, shaped him on the way to language. In fact it all-but erased him; for, as my friend reminds me, 'the logic of conversion is that the "I" is sacrificed.' Conversion, you see, is the prodigal business of getting the hell out of your self. If so, 'then who or what,' cries Prodigal Mills, 'is saved?'

That is the question. Who? If not 'I' then is it 'You'? Perhaps, for this book is forever thinking about you – it is written, I would say, You-toward. Here, there and everywhere, Mills writes things like: 'You know,' 'You figure,' 'Your move' – and, most tellingly, 'You win.' You, it seems, are one more funny thing that happened to Mills on the way to writing this book, perhaps the most funny. So: who are you? And are you still there? Still out there? You had better read on.

JOHN SCHAD
Lancaster

Slightly Misleading Preface by the Author

In his General Editor's Preface to this series John Schad quotes Paul de Man's observation that we do not know what reading is. Quite so. But I should rather like to know. So, in this book, I attempt to bring to light some of the thorny, puzzling and entangled processes and procedures that contribute to our sense-making activities – especially those associated with the discipline of literary criticism, with what we might think of as professional reading. This involves thinking about the ways in which other readers influence our understanding, and the ways in which theoretical concerns both shape and deform the construction of formal readings. In order to trace out what I imagine to be some of the less visited, but nonetheless definitive, edges of the discipline in its current phase (the place of the Bible and Christian interpretative traditions, for example) I have also attempted to give voice to figures that the critical process tends to silence. One of those figures, perhaps paradoxically, is the self. By which I mean that although issues of subjectivity and identity have been discussed *ad nauseam* (the fictionality of the Cartesian 'I' becoming something of a *parti pris*) in recent years, as far as I know little has ever been said about the relationship between the detached professional voice in which literature is typically discussed and the self that reads, thinks, laughs, cries, drinks tea and visits the bathroom. It is with this relationship in mind that I have woven elements of autobiography into the book as a way of exploring the relationship between the self and the discipline. Formally, generically, and methodologically the book declines to settle, since to do so would be to allow the reader to forget the process of reading in which they are engaged. I imagine the book as a kind of non-theatrical Brechtian experiment. You, implied reader, I'm sure, will imagine it otherwise.

KM
Llareggub, 2008

Acknowledgements

Alma and Isla (the prodigal daughter) must be first. Here my debts are too many and too great to say.

Particular thanks are due to Tiffany Atkinson, for providing this book with its title, and to other former colleagues at University of Wales, Aberystwyth, who listened attentively, critically and generously to my ideas – especially Peter Barry, Damian Walford Davies, Kelly Grovier, Jem Poster, Will Slocombe, Luke Thurston, and Richard Marggraf Turley.

Current colleagues at the University of Glamorgan have also had to put up with my ramblings: especial thanks here to Jane Aaron, Gavin Edwards, Alice Entwhistle, Philip Gross, Jeremy Hooker, Chris Meredith, Sheenagh Pugh, Andy Smith, Diana Wallace, Jeff Wallace, and Martin Willis.

Earlier versions of some of the material included here has appeared in the following journals: *Literature and Theology, Christianity and Literature, The Glass*. I am grateful to the editors and publishers.

As ever, I am indebted to John Schad – not only as series editor, but also as friend, mentor, and profound influence.

I have dedicated the book to those fine prodigals – my sister, Caris, and my brother, Vic – again, my debt is too great to put into words.

The Critical Inventions Series

Do I dare / Disturb the universe?
(T. S. Eliot, 'The Love Song of J. Alfred Prufrock', 1917)

In 1961 C. S. Lewis published *An Experiment in Criticism*; over forty years later, at the beginning of a new century, there is pressing need for a renewed sense of experiment, or invention in criticism. The energies unleashed by the theoretical movements of the 1970s and 1980s have been largely exhausted – many now say we are experiencing life after theory; some, indeed, say we are experiencing life after criticism. Criticism, we might say, is in crisis. But that is where it should be; the word 'criticism' comes, as we know, from the word 'crisis'.

Talk of crisis does not, though, fit easily within the well-managed contemporary academy; with its confident talk of 'scholarly excellence', there is a presumption that we all know, and are agreed upon, what scholarship and criticism is. However, to echo Paul de Man, 'we don't even know what reading is'; and what is, potentially, exciting about our present crisis is that now we really know that we don't know what reading is. It is, then, in a spirit of learned ignorance that we propose 'critical inventions', a series which will feature books that, in one way or another, push the generic conventions of literary criticism to breaking point. In so doing the very figure of the critic will shift and change. We shall, no doubt, glimpse something of what Oscar Wilde famously called 'the critic as artist', or what Terry Eagleton called 'the critic as clown'; we may even glimpse still more unfamiliar figures – the critic as, for example, autobiographer, novelist, mourner, poet, parodist, detective, dreamer, diarist, flaneûr, surrealist, priest, montagist, gambler, traveller, beggar, anarchist… or even amateur. In short, this series seeks the truly critical critic – or, to be paradoxical, the critic as critic; the critic who is a critic of criticism as conventionally understood, or misunderstood. He or she is the critic who will dare to disturb the universe, or at least the university – in particular, the institutionalisation of criticism that is professional, university English.

Establishment English is, though, a strange institution that is capable of disestablishing itself, if only because it houses the still stranger institution of literature – which, as Jacques Derrida once wrote, 'in principle allows us to say everything/ anything [tout dire]'. We, therefore, do not or cannot yet know of what criticism may yet be capable – capable of being, capable of doing. 'Critical inventions' will be a series that seeks to find out.

Read the text right and emancipate the world.
(Robert Browning, 'Bishop Bloughram's Apology', 1855)

JOHN SCHAD, Series Editor

. . . there never was a true story which could not be told in parables
(GEORGE ELIOT, *Middlemarch*)

Home is a place where we have not yet been
(ERNST BLOCH, *The Principle of Hope*)

Mae hen wlad fy nhadau yn annwyl i mi
(*Welsh National Anthem*)

What we start with Fathers –
what we both know about –
How's yer? – Who's yer? – and
the old lines of begats.
(TIFFANY ATKINSON, 'Four Poems For, III')

Am I not father, too . . .
(DYLAN THOMAS, 'Do You Not Father Me')

Over the door
In invisible letters there is the name:
Home, but it is no place
to return to.
(R. S. THOMAS, 'Grandparents')

The Gospel According to St Luke, chapter 15 (King James Version)

[1] Then drew near unto him all the publicans and sinners for to hear him.

[2] And the Pharisees and scribes murmured, saying, This man receiveth sinners, and eateth with them.

[3] And he spake this parable unto them, saying,

[4] What man of you, having an hundred sheep, if he lose one of them, doth not leave the ninety and nine in the wilderness, and go after that which is lost, until he find it?

[5] And when he hath found it, he layeth it on his shoulders, rejoicing.

[6] And when he cometh home, he calleth together his friends and neighbours, saying unto them, Rejoice with me; for I have found my sheep which was lost.

[7] I say unto you, that likewise joy shall be in heaven over one sinner that repenteth, more than over ninety and nine just persons, which need no repentance.

[8] Either what woman having ten pieces of silver, if she lose one piece, doth not light a candle, and sweep the house, and seek diligently till she find it?

[9] And when she hath found it, she calleth her friends and her neighbours together, saying, Rejoice with me; for I have found the piece which I had lost.

[10] Likewise, I say unto you, there is joy in the presence of the angels of God over one sinner that repenteth.

[11] And he said, A certain man had two sons:

[12] And the younger of them said to his father, Father, give me the portion of goods that falleth to me. And he divided unto them his living.

[13] And not many days after the younger son gathered all together, and took his journey into a far country, and there wasted his substance with riotous living.

[14] And when he had spent all, there arose a mighty famine in that land; and he began to be in want.

[15] And he went and joined himself to a citizen of that country; and he sent him into his fields to feed swine.

[16] And he would fain have filled his belly with the husks that the swine did eat: and no man gave unto him.

[17] And when he came to himself, he said, How many hired servants of my father's have bread enough and to spare, and I perish with hunger!

[18] I will arise and go to my father, and will say unto him, Father, I have sinned against heaven, and before thee,

[19] And am no more worthy to be called thy son: make me as one of thy hired servants.

²⁰ And he arose, and came to his father. But when he was yet a great way off, his father saw him, and had compassion, and ran, and fell on his neck, and kissed him.

²¹ And the son said unto him, Father, I have sinned against heaven, and in thy sight, and am no more worthy to be called thy son.

²² But the father said to his servants, Bring forth the best robe, and put it on him; and put a ring on his hand, and shoes on his feet:

²³ And bring hither the fatted calf, and kill it; and let us eat, and be merry:

²⁴ For this my son was dead, and is alive again; he was lost, and is found. And they began to be merry.

²⁵ Now his elder son was in the field: and as he came and drew nigh to the house, he heard musick and dancing.

²⁶ And he called one of the servants, and asked what these things meant.

²⁷ And he said unto him, Thy brother is come; and thy father hath killed the fatted calf, because he hath received him safe and sound.

²⁸ And he was angry, and would not go in: therefore came his father out, and intreated him.

²⁹ And he answering said to his father, Lo, these many years do I serve thee, neither transgressed I at any time thy commandment: and yet thou never gavest me a kid, that I might make merry with my friends:

³⁰ But as soon as this thy son was come, which hath devoured thy living with harlots, thou hast killed for him the fatted calf.

³¹ And he said unto him, Son, thou art ever with me, and all that I have is thine.

³² It was meet that we should make merry, and be glad: for this thy brother was dead, and is alive again; and was lost, and is found.

Introduction

GHOST   I am thy father's spirit.
Hamlet, Act 1, scene 5

I feel the need of an escapade after these serious . . . books whose form is always so closely considered. I want to kick up my heels and be off. I want to embody all those innumerable little ideas and tiny stories which flash into my mind at all seasons.[1]

1. Kick up Your Heels

The critic, sitting down to write, wants to make a text out of innumerable little ideas and tiny stories that have amassed as the residue of professional activity. I was going to say 'wants to make sense' of these minutiae, but making sense is not necessarily the aim; making an argument, possibly; constructing a convincing performance, almost certainly. But often, just below the surface of what we must call the discipline, is the need for an escapade – a strong desire to shuck off scholarly constraints, to kick up the heels and be off. For Woolf, it was the transgendered Orlando that provided the vehicle for her excursion, and perhaps the desire for escape always has some kind of a gender implication. For it is something like the law of the father that there should be a discipline, and the law of the father is the mother of resistance.

2. Father Repressor

Luce Irigarary writes:

Desire for her, her desire, that is what is forbidden by the law of the father, of all fathers: fathers of families, fathers of nations, religious fathers, professor-fathers, doctor-fathers, lover-fathers, etc. Moral or immoral, they always intervene to censor, to repress, the desire of/for the mother. For them, that corresponds to good sense and good health, when it's not virtue and sainthood![2]

But I am a father. A father in search of, in need of, an escapade from serious books, yet held in thrall by the paternity, the patriarchy even, that defines me. The repressor repressed. How can the law of the father be resisted by the (male) child who is, as Wordsworth says, 'the father to the man', and who thus embodies the closed circle of (a) discipline? Only in stories. For, it is only in stories that male roles are multiple; only in stories can a father also be a lover, a son, a servant, and a brother. By which I mean that there is always that in syntax that exceeds the order of the sign; there is always that in narrative that is unassimilable in theory.

3. The Lore of the Father

I teach you the lore of the father: the story of the prodigal son.

4. Desire

In *The Madwoman in the Attic*, Gilbert and Gubar showed us that the myth of the textual father has a long history and a deep shadow. As they point out, generations of male writers have arrogated to their gender the power of the phallic pen, to the extent that the western tradition has equated writing with maleness, with paternity, with the 'generative power of the penis'.[3] Harold Bloom's account of influence, they remind us, is a story of fathers and sons, of sons seeking to overcome their fathers. But if Irigaray is right, then to run from the father is also to express the desire of/for the mother.

The story of the prodigal son seems both germane and inadequate: the son seeks to escape his father's influence; he runs away in order to build on the inheritance he has acquired at the father's expense; then he returns and is welcomed back by the father. But the mother is nowhere to be seen in the parable. She must, we imagine, be present as desire. So, even when the tradition closes around its sons, re-absorbs them into the male line, somewhere in the background is the unrepresented, unreflected mother, silent as a mirror.

5. Fiction

We find her, Gilbert and Gubar say, in transit between worlds: in order to escape the distorted image of themselves reflected in male texts, women have to 'journey through the looking glass toward literary autonomy.'[4] Here the parable bends like a concave reflection. The woman, like the son, must escape the law of the father, but she *must not* return. Her absence from the parable, then, may be a good thing: maybe she has passed beyond it into the field of the unreflected where male distortions cannot twist her. But we will not forget her because she has made the story possible. Paternity, Gilbert and Gubar remind us, is a 'legal fiction' but it is one enabled, if not necessitated, by maternity. This means that when stories exclude the mother, they do so as the printed word neglects to mention the pen, the paper and the ink.

6. Escape and Return

Since prodigality is by definition both following and not following, it is parabolic in relation to the nexus of the critical and creative. The creative gesture, even as part of the critical process by which we seek out the new in the old, is one of escape, of wanting not to repeat, of espousing, craving, or imagining discontinuity. The desire of/for the mother, maybe. But it is also a matter of return, of continuation and repetition.

7. Anxieties

In one sense, *The Prodigal Sign* is about the anxiety of criticism. In part, this is what Harold Bloom famously termed 'the anxiety of influence' – the nagging doubt that we may be doing nothing that has not been done before. But it is also the anxiety of ignorance – the need to prove our scholarly credentials, our familiarity with the work in our particular field of endeavour. We need to show that we know enough or have done enough to make our work worthwhile. It is also, of course, the anxiety of indolence: the fear engendered by the scale of the task. And, maybe, it is the anxiety of impotence: the fear that we cannot father a viable text.

8. Influence

The prodigal son is a victim of all of these anxieties. He fears the influence of home and family on his freedom of mind and spirit; he does too little to be satisfied with his lot; he is ignorant of what awaits him out in the wide world. He creates nothing, for the father provides. These anxieties are not ameliorated by his escape attempt; they return to haunt him, and they drive him home again, but for how long no-one knows.

9. The Burden of the Past

W. Jackson Bate's *The Burden of the Past* dealt with the problem of how a poet finds a place in relationship to those who have gone before, with how to establish one's own place in a European / English tradition.[5] In Bate's account of poetics and the relations holding between poets, it is almost as if that tradition is imagined to operate according to some kind of periodic table of poets. There seem to be only so many slots available, and each is occupied by a single poet who is directly related to those next to them in a closed system or structure of artistic density. One can find such ideas at work in the belletrist criticism of Edmund Gosse, and in the T. S. Eliot of 'Tradition and the Individual Talent'. Such approaches have, of course, long since been superseded by theories of intertextuality and intersubjectivity. One way of thinking the prodigal is as a different mode of address to what precedes and succeeds us: neither influence nor intertextuality alone, but prodigality: escape that is also return; following that is also not following: the juncture that is disjuncture; the nest of interwoven anxieties. I am speaking of critics. Or of poets.

10. Alterations of (Ker)Mode

Frank Kermode tells us that in the business of the interpretation of texts, 'there are alterations of mode caused by the need to make one's seniors seem obsolete.'[6] I would like my book to make others seem obsolete, just as they have done to their forebears. But I am not committed to their obsolescence; I also want them to stand because I recognise a symmetry that is possibly ethical. I am a father as well as a son.

11. The Inheritance

As Bate and Bloom both know, and Kermode knows it too, originality is the problem of modernity, in critical as well as in creative writing. We all know now that there is no such thing: all is intertextual, intersubjective, parasitic, symbiotic. Yet, even today, we sign our books, and we invite the august author to speak on the basis of what we have read under the sign of their name. Even today, to call a work 'original' sounds like the highest praise. It is a myth we live by. But originality is, inevitably, comparative – recognised only in relation to what has gone before, in comparison with what it both follows and does not follow. It lives on the inheritance that it seeks to possess, purports to escape, and inevitably consumes.

12. Funding

Escape is always funded by inheritance.

13. The Lost

The new is always a repetition. Bloom tells us as much. The parable of the prodigal son is itself a new repetition – a story that repeats and alters the others by which it is framed and which it also frames: the stories of the lost sheep and of the lost coin. To be new is to repeat, but also to be lost, not to know quite where one is or where one has come from, or where one is going. Return seems inevitable since any act of orientation or of locating oneself is the rediscovery of the familiar in the unfamiliar.

14. Home

In *The Times Higher Education Supplement* dated January 2007, Derek Attridge and Jane Elliott wrote: 'If theory is increasingly fragmented, at odds with its own beginnings, perhaps that is only to be expected.' Theory was never about providing a stable background for critical practice. Theorists were ever at odds with themselves. Necessarily, since it is the basic premise of the theoretical project 'that when we go back to the beginning, we never find it as stable or coherent as we had hoped; the ground on which we stand always turns out to be crumbling beneath our feet.'[7] The prodigal's return is never to an unchanged, unchanging, or secure home. Rather, it is, paradoxically, to the new: to a situation that is both familiar and unfamiliar at the same time. As Ernst Bloch once wrote: 'Home is a place we have not yet been'.[8] Living and writing on after theory, we know how this feels.

15. The Sound Heard Only in the Echo

When I announced to some colleagues that my next book would be entitled *The Prodigal Sign*, one of them suggested that it sounded like an echo
of the 1980s – a return to the days of high theoretical fervour. It was, of
course, the presence of the word 'sign', recalling those poststructuralist
years when every text turned out to be about 'language itself', that
prompted the remark. It is hardly surprising that I should adopt a title with
such resonance since I grew up intellectually during the years of the theory
boom, learned my critical theory at the feet of Christopher Norris, and
devoted my first book to the problems of representation associated with the
deconstruction of the Saussurean sign. I have never been quite sure what to
do since then.

16. *Inter Alia*

This book is – *inter alia* – about that uncertainty. It arises out of a sense that
deconstruction (I do not mean by this term generic poststructuralism) was
never defeated. We grew tired of it, that's all, and ran away. The problems
it highlighted, exposed or unearthed were intractable, so we side-stepped
them and went back to doing history, cultural criticism, various kinds of
formalism, or whatever else our inclinations led to, in a slightly more self-
conscious, self-critical way than we had before.

17. Practice and Principle

It is easy to grow tired of theory. Of any particular theory, anyway. I imagine that this is due partly to the boredom induced by repetition and
familiarity, and partly to a subconscious acknowledgement that any reflection on our own practice reveals the inconsistencies, the detours or
swerves, the moments at which our thinking or our reading betrays its
unwillingness to remain true to the principles we espouse. Deconstruction
is of particular interest in this sense because it is predicated upon the
insight that, as Derrida observed, no practice is ever entirely true to its
principles, and because it is very difficult not to exceed the deconstructive
demand that we should not import into our reading of a text any kind of
extrinsic (and therefore discontinuous), methodology, context, or predis-
position.

As any prodigal will tell you, it is not easy to feel at home in the detour; it is the critical equivalent of feeding swine for a living.

18. The Job

In interpretations of the story of the prodigal son, too little attention is paid to the time the eponymous lad spends doing a worthwhile job rather than loafing in his dad's swanky home. This period is usually understood as a detour, an error, a precursor and necessary condition to repentance and return. It is as if the work he did was of no account. But swine will always need feeding, and I am quite fond of pigs.

19. Double Failure

The application of the adjective 'prodigal' to the noun 'sign' is a self-conscious echo of a critical past that I have failed to escape, but to which I have failed to be true. This is the sign of the prodigal – this double failure that evokes the parable of the prodigal son. This is a book about the prodigal acts of attempting to run away from fathers, precursors, histories, influences, academic practices, institutions, oneself.

20. Mythologies

Mostly this is about the Bible as a text that captured me in my childhood and from which I cannot escape. It is about running away and returning. In deploying the story of the prodigal, I do not mean to suggest that escape and return is a necessary pattern or a predetermined order. I am not a fatalist. I offer it merely as a hypothesis, a model that might be tested as a way of thinking about theory now. In a recent exchange on this issue, I was challenged on precisely this point. The counter-case is that critical discourses *do* make real advances; escapes have been made without return – the feminist, the postcolonial, the queer. One might need do no more than change the mythology, the argument goes, apply a classical typology rather than a Christian one.

But, as Freud has shown us all too clearly, classical mythology does not offer us any clean breaks. Those father-killers of classical antiquity who sought to overthrow the control systems that bound them, suffered their own kinds of return, as repressed deeds turned into ongoing pathologies. In fact, our language of return is derived more from those myths than from the Christian: Oedipus, Elektra, Odysseus, Achilles.

21. Advancing

I do not deny that real change, real advance, is possible. But even genuine advances, the production of changed political and interpretative situations, involve certain kinds of technical return in the sense that their stories can be and have been told as narratives of escape, of discontinuity, and, as I argue in 'Reason's Disciple,' there is no such thing as undifferentiated or pure discontinuity; the break is always a repetition and a return. To tell the story is, necessarily, in some sense, to recuperate the break, to assimilate it to an order that is in certain ways familiar and repeated.

22. To Read the Reader

Such an insight could be thought of as itself a kind of return to a specifi-cally Christian hermeneutic in the sense that it repeats the prodigal's journey, placing the archetypal narrative of repentance and conversion at the heart of the critical project. In *Prodigal Son / Elder Brother*, Jill Robbins points out that the story of the prodigal son has long been afforded the status of a privileged allegory of the hermeneutical venture:

> the prodigal son's journey – a movement of departure from and return to home and self – figures the very detour to the self that constitutes Christian hermeneutics and its economy of salvation. It underwrites all narratives of personal conversion, whether they be exemplary, like Augustine's, or belated, as in the case of Petrarch. So central is the prodigal son's story to the Christian imagination, describing as it does God's mercy toward sinners, that it has been called 'the Gospel in the Gospel'.[9]

Robbins' assessment is just: Christian hermeneutics always implies defec-tion, repentance, conversion: the process of arriving at a meaning for the text is also the process of allowing the text to read the reader. The encounter issues in the emergence of both a meaning for the text and a new self-understanding for the interpreter: text and reader return to them-selves. But the story of the prodigal could always be read differently: as a story that contains the seeds of other stories that are not assimilable to the conversion narrative.

23. Short Circuit

Another way of thinking the return in the contemporary situation is in terms of what deconstruction demanded (or demands), and the inevitability of our return to something less insistently watchful, less intense, less demanding of infinite linguistic self-scrutiny. If escaping, or expressing a desire to escape, or consciously resisting, questioning, or problematising logocentrism, phallogocentrism, ontotheology, the metaphysics of presence and so on, required us to make endless detours, to never arrive at meaning, context, history, the presence of our subject, then we have indeed returned, not to the same situation, but to the same territory – albeit in a refurbished condition – that deconstruction once bade us leave. We no longer feel the detour to be endless. We have decided, realistically or otherwise, that the circuits of language and representation can be shorted without any loss of power.

24. Narrative and Concept

My deployment of the term 'prodigal' is itself prodigal: it refuses to be pinned down. This is not only because the sign of the prodigal indicates detour, exorbitance, irresponsibility and so on, but also because it stands for a narrative that cannot be reduced to a conceptual content or framework. 'The Prodigal Son' is a story as well as being a character; it takes in, elaborates or envisages more than one role or persona, and the trajectory of the prodigal's journey is not the only narrative arc that can be traced through it. Christian interpretations of it have always focused on the prodigal himself, and on the father who welcomes him home, seeing in the tale of defection, repentance and homecoming, the archetypal conversion story.

But others, standing outside the Christian tradition, have seen less easily assimilated elements. I am thinking, principally, of Robbins' reading. She reads the parable as a narrative of interpretative exclusion, focusing on the role of the elder brother who refuses to rejoice at the prodigal's safe return. Here, the elder brother is the excluded Jew, relegated to the sidelines by Christian salvation history. It is not difficult to see why this conclusion has been reached, given that, as Robbins observes: 'the Lukean text invites this reading because of the structural position and image of the Pharisees in relation to Jesus' parables, namely, as an audience whose alleged self-righteousness the parable criticises and reproaches.'[10] Furthermore,

Augustine's influential gloss on the parable, upon which Robbins is commenting, insists upon seeing the elder brother in this light.

25. Come Outside

One could always argue that such an interpretation could be turned against Augustine's excoriation of the Jew, by pointing to the father's response to the elder son's complaint that his own faithfulness has gone unappreciated and unrewarded: the father insists upon the firstborn's continued primacy in the family business: 'all that I have is yours'. The prodigal may get a party, but his inheritance is gone, and the elder son will lose nothing by the whole affair; he will, sooner or later, have the last laugh. Curiously, this is part of neither Augustine's Christian thinking, nor Robbins' resistant, critical response to it. Robbins focuses instead on the exteriority of the elder son, his outsider status, picking up on the way in which 'New Testament' scholars such as Julius Wellhausen and Dan Via seem content to read him out of the story.[11] He thus becomes a figure of the unsaid, or the excluded, or the marginalised, of the kind that so delighted the critics of twenty years ago. But, of course, to valorise the marginal is also to change its status to something more central, and therefore less worthy of our sympathy or our scrutiny. What interests me in this context is that while the parable does keep the grumpy brother outside, it also has the father leave the celebrations and come outside to speak with him, in a special effort not only to include him in the party, but also to reinforce his familial cachet as the elder son. So, he might appear to have a status that outbids his brother's momentary celebrity; he is certainly neither disregarded nor even relegated to nonentity as far as the parable itself is concerned, even if that was the effect of the Christian interpretation of the parable following Augustine. In our rejection of Christian hermeneutics, of course, in following the lead of the Jew, we have all moved outside to join the elder brother. In this sense we have followed the prodigal father who leaves home in order to expand the borders of the domestic, who breaches the walls to heal the wound.

26. Old and New

At stake in this conflict of interpretations surrounding the respective positions of the prodigal son and his elder brother are a number of crucial issues that are of great significance for literary criticism. In the first place, this has to do with the fact that, as Robbins shows, the parable is the *locus classicus* of Christian hermeneutics in action. It forms a cathexis in Augustine's work – a textual space in which are concentrated the theological, philosophical, and analogical energies that came to animate not only his own critical practice, but that of a whole interpretative tradition. So much so that the parable still invites the Christian reader to make figures that render experience intelligible in narrative terms, and to locate human finitude, fallibility and longing in relation to self-realisation, acceptance and homecoming. But it also allows us to see that the figural patterns that make experience intelligible are determined by the framework within which they are constructed. We might read the elder brother out of the story, or we might read him into it, and we might read these readings as readings of reading. By which I mean that the elder son as figure of the Jew, also stands for the Hebrew Bible christened as the 'Old Testament', and as such he foregrounds our tendency to make figures, to interpret figurally. For that tendency originates in the will to make the 'Old' a figure of the 'New' – the older a figure of the younger: our own interpretative practice an antitype to that of our predecessors.

27. Synthetype

But, at the risk of returning to Hegel, every antitype is also a synthetype: a type on the next level of the spiral of interpretations.

28. Who do You think You Are?

Beyond the horizon of such histories (in which the prodigal thrives while his brother languishes, or the Christian shuts out the Jew), there is another way of reading that seeks to do justice to or with the text. We need to put ourselves into the story in order to uncover it, remembering that we may be (or may have) sisters as well as brothers, mothers as well as fathers, and that there are servants, possibly even slaves, in the house who will inherit nothing. That is to say, the parable of the prodigal son tells us a story that might, in certain ways, be our own, but that we are not limited by the roles prescribed for us.

29. (Non-)Participant Roles

We might follow the story, or not follow it. But of course, not to follow the story is to follow the prodigal in his flight, to stand outside with the elder brother, to leave the party with the father, or not to participate, like the mother.

30. Mum

It was my mother who (before I could read) first told me the story of the prodigal son.

Parable and Criticism
The Prodigal Son

Before the work begins, if it has not begun already, I will tell you straight: I aspire to prodigality. I do not mean that I love waste; I have too much of the protestant manqué about me for that. No. I mean that I like to imagine myself disapproved of by others, especially by Bible critics and new historicists. It is a fantasy, I know, because some of my best friends are Bible critics and some are new historicists. In a sense this is the fantasy of all criticism: to say the unassimilable, to think the heretical, to run away from the founders and the fathers. Nonetheless, I am keen to disavow the relationship between texts and history that fascinates both disciplinary schools, both because history is a tyrant that ruins reading in the present moment, and because it is a matter for scholars. I turn to parable because it is the antithesis of history, and because it perplexes Bible critics.

If nothing else does, what I have to say about servants will piss them off, I'm sure. Why? Because I am not – for the moment – interested in historical authenticity, philological accuracy, or the recovery of discursive contexts. The word 'servant', in this context, means only what it means in this context. 'Ah', you will say: 'What if the word translated "servant" in the English versions of the Bible, actually meant "giraffe", and the giraffe was a totemic animal? Would you not need to know that fact?' Well . . . no, actually. I am fairly confident that 'servant' no longer means 'giraffe'. Furthermore, even if I know that 'servant' once meant 'giraffe', I have no access to the meaning of 'giraffe' in its historical and cultural context. I cannot know in any more than a superficial way how first-century hearers of parables felt about, thought about, or related to giraffes. And anyway, to generalise about first-century hearers of parables would be no less productive of inaccuracy than to misread 'giraffe' as 'servant'.

What, for example, would it do to the relation between the original meaning of 'giraffe' and our construction of it, had there been a whole genre of giraffe jokes in circulation that were never written down, and about which we had never even heard? We have certainly not heard, nor could we ever hear, everything of the past. Or what if there had been an oral folk tale of the giraffe who invested wisely, circulating at the time when the parable of the talents was first told? To what extent might such unknown contexts have hidden from us the connotations of the word? What if there had been a giraffe kicking the shit out of an aged servant behind the speaker's back when the parable of the unmerciful giraffe was first told? Would that not have had an impact on the original meaning of the story to its first hearers? Contextualisation always lies because it does not know what it does not know about the past, but it forgets to say so.

My point is that history in all its limitless, unruly, unmasterable, layered, multiple, rich, diverse, unknowable, messy depth, darkness and complexity is never going to be a reliable guide to meanings past or present. Meaning was never any less context-dependent than it is now, and contexts are not recoverable in any but the most attenuated and deceptive form. I tend to agree with that prodigal son of the Enlightenment, Johann Georg Hamann:

> But can one know the past when one does not even understand the present? And who can have right ideas of the present without knowing the future? The future determines the present, and the present determines the past . . . The field of history has always seemed to me to be like that wide field that was full of bones, and behold, they were very dry. Only a prophet can prophesy of these bones that veins and flesh will grow on them and skin cover them. They still have no breath in them till the prophet prophesies to the wind and the word of the Lord speaks to the wind . . . [1]

Until the prophets return, history is bones.

Then there is the difficulty that is presented by the fact that I am unable to divest myself of my own (extremely limited) experience of giraffes and the ways in which that experience has influenced what happens in my head when I encounter the word 'giraffe'. Nor can I escape the conditions under which I read about giraffes, any more than I can ascertain the conditions under which they were written or spoken about in the past: whether I am well or ill, happy or miserable, in bed or at a bus stop, thirsty, in need of a toilet, hot, cold, tired, bored, irritated, amused, skittish, serious, distracted, worried and so on. Even where they are known, the effects on meaning of these conditions of production and consumption are unquantifiable.

The giraffe is a parable that was told to me by Gavin Edwards.

I. The Parabolic Problem

Parables are tricky things; especially those associated with Jesus. They defy definition and explanation, and cause problems for interpreters, whether their interests are theological or literary. In the first place parables raise the thorny issue of authorship, of what is attributable to the evangelist and what to the subject of his discourse. How can the words of Jesus be extricated from framing narratives and interpretative pericopes? This problem is heightened by the existence of discrepancies between the gospels: variant versions of a parable can differ significantly from one gospel to another, not only in the specific details of actors, actions and occurrences, but also in terms of a parable's place in the larger narrative pattern.

The parables also divide biblical critics between those who think that attention should be paid to the text as a literary artefact and those who see the text as a vehicle for historical transmission: one might be in search of the historical Jesus, hoping to see through the text to a bygone age, while another is interested in the theological or authorial characteristics of Matthew, Mark, Luke or John.[2]

Again, the study of the parables of Jesus has had to confront a profound interpretative dichotomy: is a parable a realistic narrative with a recoverable *sitz im leben*, as has been argued by the likes of Adolph Julicher, Joachim Jeremias, and C.H. Dodd ? Or is it best understood as a mystifying allegory of salvation history, as assumed by the long tradition of Christian interpretation coming down from Augustine and Origen? Another approach circumvents the question and insists that a parable should be read as a 'speech event', independent of historical context; such was the contention of practitioners of the self-styled New Hermeneutic, such as Ernst Fuchs and Gerhard Ebeling.[3]

No matter which approach one takes, there are residual questions and problems that seem to demand supplementation from a contrary critical perspective. If we follow the realists, then we find that insistent allegorical patterns that turn participants into figures of spiritual or moral value, have to be explained away by means of linguistic contortions, by attributing the tendency to the interpretative interpolations of the evangelists and the theological interests of the early church, or by ignoring the extent to which the genre derived certain of its allegorical functions from the Hebrew *mashal*. The latter is itself is a difficult tradition to pin down: 'the word "Mashal" and its synonyms, which underlie the "parabolé" of the gospels, cover a wide range of utterance, varying from, at the one end, the brief and self-explanatory proverb, through manifold forms of extended metaphor to, at the other end – and this is most surprising – the riddle or enigma'. [4] So, while the prehistory of the parable might seem essential to establishing the generic parameters within which particular instances of the form are to be read, the specific interpretation of the tradition that is operative in the formation of any given parable is not easily determined. Deciding upon the realism of a parable, then, may depend upon a set of linguistically and culturally complex issues that in themselves bring to light prevenient and far more intractable interpretative problems associated with translation, transmission, and historical currency.

If we eschew the realist mode and elect to read parables allegorically, then we have to puzzle out what could have motivated the drive to encrypt ideas, mores and injunctions rather than expressing them in more literal, more direct terms. The assertion that parabolic encodings can be attributed to a kind of gnostic tendency that sought to create a spiritual elite on the basis of cultic initiation, leaves us to wonder at the ease with which the code can, at times, be broken, and why the parables of Jesus often focus on familiar, everyday activities and procedures such as fishing, growing crops, attending wedding feasts and so on. It can readily be observed that the apocalyptists showed far greater facility in the creation of encoded revelations; by comparison with the books of Daniel and Revelation, the parables appear exemplary in their realism and lucidity. Even the writer of Mark's gospel, often considered to be the propagator of the so-called 'messianic secret', is torn between the insistence upon a Jesus who reveals his secret kingdom to a select few, and a Jesus whose words are designed to address the common people in familiar terms.[5]

Again, to focus on the parable as a 'speech event' leaves out of consideration the irreducible textuality of parables as they come down to us, and the stripping away of historical specificity implicit in the procedure simply raises the question of genre and its significance for our pre-understanding. Generic expectations, conscious or not, shape our approach to all texts, and genre is never free of history any more than is an 'event', whether spoken or enacted. But then history is as elusive as parable itself when it comes to locating a context or a set of particular conditions lying behind the text, since history is not in any sufficiently determinate way, its mode of existence, as Gerald Bruns has acutely observed of Scripture in general: 'what is at issue with respect to the Scriptures is not what lies behind the text in the form of an original meaning, but what lies in front of it where the interpreter stands.'[6] Even if we disregard the assumption that 'Scriptures', as texts privileged or distinguished by a normative tradition, deserve their own distinct hermeneutical protocols, the point remains, for there is no place for a text to be other than 'where the interpreter stands'. History always lags behind interpretation for this reason; it is never up to date, for the interpreter's time has yet to be written. Parabolic utterance brings this into focus both because it refuses to belong to a time (it is like myth in this sense – it addresses the hearer/reader without limits), and because it both raises the question of genre and, at the same time, resists its constraints.

David Parris has argued that parable problematises generic attribution by virtue of its mimetic qualities, its staging of the coalescence of internal and external representation. Following Alasdair MacIntyre, Parris uses the term 'internal representation' to denote the features or characteristics that belong intrinsically to a picture or image, while 'external representation' refers to similarities between the picture or image and something outside of it.[7] Intervening in the old debate about whether or not parables are allegories, Parris argues that they cannot be reduced to the bipolar terms of this distinction since they contain both recognisably decode-able images and internally coherent narrative form. That is to say: since parables at times nudge and wink at the hearer/reader, hinting at pre-existing symbolic values, while at the same time offering stories that do not depend upon such a code for their narrative coherence, they are never reducible to any unitary or unambiguous generic category. He concludes:

> The distinction between parable and allegory is not always clear . . . the different classifications of genre we apply to the parables are derivative. They should be assigned after we have participated in the mimetic representation of the parable. To declare that the parables are allegories or that they are non-allegorical is to cast a net in advance. As a result, the possible field of mimetic play is reduced and the a priori categories with which we approach them will determine to a large extent what we find in the parables.[8]

I would argue that we are *never* in the position of *having participated* in the mimetic representation of the parable; the story continues; it never resolves itself into the meaning produced by either an allegorical deciphering, or a moment of recognition in the grasping of a similitude. It is the peculiarity of narrative to exceed conceptualisation, to leave a remnant that is not assimilable within a single interpretative discourse. Therefore, the problem of genre is incapable of solution. In the continuous time of the interpreter, we are always *in medias res*. Parables elude us because we can never arrive at the place of attribution; we cannot step outside the story in order to name it, any more than we can be done with mimesis.

It is just this intractability of parables that makes them appealing in the contemporary situation. Those associated with the teaching of Jesus have been in circulation in western cultures for hundreds of years, and so they have a familiarity, albeit a diminishing one, that makes them public property in a way matched by few other texts. For this reason, they bring us up sharply against the challenges of received meaning, of multivalency, of over-determination, of the interface between religious meaning and critical response. But they also evoke the *desire* to find meanings in stories that transcend the shape of the narrative and the specificities of its articulation. To quote one commentator: 'Parables defy precise doctrine or moral interpretation; or, more infuriatingly still, admit it only on the level of moral commonplace, escaping all our attempts to articulate the more profound and numinous meanings which we feel to be obscurely present in them.'[9] Defying theological meaning, infuriating those in search of transcendent presences, parables could almost appear to be expressions of the postmodern impatience with fixity, definition or finality. It is no coincidence that among the writers who appealed most strongly to critics of a 'postmodern' persuasion were creators of parables: Kafka, Borges, Kierkegaard.

But parables also have a contrary appeal. As Bernard Harrison suggests, there is something about parables that makes us *want* those passé things – the profound, the numinous, the transcendent – or that at least prompts us to imagine that there might be recoverable traces of them in the parabolic form. It is the 'obscure presence', illusory or not, that titillates. The play of hiddenness and openness, responsible for this teasing effect, is characteristic of narrative in general, but it takes on an especial significance in certain parables, because, as John Drury observes, they occupy a liminal position that intensifies the sense of suspension, prolonging the deferral of closure, maintaining the moment of potentiality:

> Narrative engages its readers by feeding them a mixture of the hidden and the open. We are told enough to get us interested because we understand it. Enough is kept back from us to keep us interested by the presence of things which we do not understand, but hope to understand by reading on or reading again more carefully. It happens horizontally, along the story line: how will it end? . . . It also happens vertically: what is the deep and mysterious ground or source of these events which I am reading about? When parables occur in narratives they, as parts of the story, share these properties. As stories within the story they take stock of its movement along the line of time by reflecting, from the moment in between which they occupy, on the past, which has been told, and the future, which has yet to be told. They work vertically too. The space occupied by a parable is a temporary halt in the narration which is used to explore the depth and ground of what is past and impending.[10]

Drury's description is a powerful one because it suggests that the parabolic intervention opens up narrative to its own limits, exposing it to its own logic by simultaneously continuing and discontinuing the progress. It involves narrative in a self-reflexive engagement: the narrative within a narrative, a parable disrupts narrative by drawing attention to it. Each time it occurs there is a momentary seizure, a spot of time that takes the reader out of the broader narrative without severance. It is a following that does not follow: anacoluthon.

Another way of thinking about the challenge presented by parables, about their ability to open troublesome or disconcerting interpretative possibilities, emerges from Harrison's previously mentioned account of the parables of Jesus. It seems to me to be amongst the most interesting of recent times precisely because it deals with a crucial dimension of the hermeneutical strangeness I have been trying to evoke. He sees Jesus' parables as *narrative* interventions in *critical/conceptual* debates: they are difficult to pin down because they are designed to question or problematise the terms and frames of reference of those who resist the kingdom. In other words, their function is argumentative:

> Dodd and Jeremias both see the parables as *arguments*, or rather as moves in a polemic. They point out that parables are often a reply to a questioner, who may be openly hostile. . . . But parables are of course not 'arguments' in the sense of sets of propositional premises entailing conclusions which confute opposing *propositions*.[11]

The parables emerge as interventions in debate that indicate a refusal to accept the grounds upon which argument is engaged; they confront arguments or propositions with narrative, and Harrison asks why this should be the case. His answer is that 'parabolic narrative has as one of its functions the subversion of the conceptual scheme in terms of which its hearers construe the world and their lives in it.'[12]

On this account, the parable is the point at which the critical meets the creative, and vice versa.

Harrison makes his case in readings of three parables, one of which is the parable of the prodigal son. For obvious reasons, this is the one I will use to recount his argument. After retelling the parable in his own words, Harrison offers this reading of it:

> . . . the father's behaviour makes nonsense of common considerations of fairness and justice in the management of family affairs. The younger son has made all the claims on the estate he has a right to make . . . . In terms of the ordinary reciprocal rights and duties of parents and children, and ordinary considerations of justice in the disposition of an estate between different members of a family, the parable is a story of a besotted old fool. But we cannot take this as its point, because the father's reply to his son is clearly

supposed to be in some way a telling one; and in any case the parable is offered as illuminating the nature of the Kingdom of Heaven.[13]

The reply of father to son in question is found in Luke 15: 31–2: 'Son, you are always with me, and all that is mine is yours . . . this your brother was dead, and is alive; he was lost and is found.' Given the requirement of contributing to an understanding of the Kingdom, and the narrative focus on the joy of a reunited family, Harrison argues, the search for the point of the parable must go further. He picks up on the fact that the prodigal returns to his father's house with the idea that he will accept the position of a servant since he has exhausted all his rights and privileges as a son. But the father has other ideas; he cannot allow his son to accept such a reduced status. Harrison continues:

> He [the father] goes, in his response, instantly beyond anything the prodigal hoped or could have hoped for. He orders up a feast, and orders the prodigal to be dressed in his best robe, because he thinks that that is the appropriate response to the situation. What, then, does he think it an appropriate response *to*? Certainly not the prodigal's *deserts*: if the feast were a feast to reward *desert* it would be a feast given for the elder son . . . . it cannot be anything which the prodigal has done or that he brings with him. Therefore it can only be the prodigal himself. *He* is the thing of great value which the father has regained, and whose recovery he is therefore celebrating. This is why the elder son's objection is peculiarly out of place . . . . In the gulf between the father's joy and the reaction of the elder son . . . we see the abyss which separates the everyday morality which we all know well enough how to handle, from the extraordinary outlook which Christ is not only recommending to us but asserting as a condition of our salvation.[14]

So, the tale of the prodigal son, in common with many other parables of Jesus, Harrison considers to be at odds with the 'underlying structures of social practices and their corresponding systems of concepts.'[15] The response Jesus makes is necessarily narrative in form because only as such can it escape the strictures of clearly defined, predetermined concepts, without refusing altogether to engage with the issues at stake. Where those strictures impinge upon the value attached to human beings in their social context, their relative worth within specific legal/political/religious formations, the significance of the parable becomes strikingly apparent. The story of the prodigal son is an intervention in just such a debate: it is framed in Luke's gospel as a response to a social judgement about the worth of 'publicans and sinners'.

Of course, Harrison's approach to the parable demands the bracketing (or the denial) of any allegorical function that parables may have. This needs to be borne in mind, for it means that wherever parable meets up with, occurs within, or troubles the texture of critical discourse, it may carry with it certain subversive potential: it may turn an argument into something other than itself. Again, Harrison's account fails to register the interest of the servants: they are, on this account, no more than objectified functionaries in a system that excludes them; they serve as the others in contrast with whom the rich, free individuals define themselves. So, while he claims that the parable 'separates the everyday morality which we all know well enough how to handle, from the extraordinary outlook which Christ is not only recommending to us but asserting as a condition of our salvation,' he fails to notice that it also replicates the everyday morality that is predicated upon economic difference and exclusion.

As Harrison's reading of the story of the prodigal son demonstrates, parables seem to never quite serve our purposes, and perhaps this is because they are, by nature, irruptions within other discourses, suasive stories in which the critical and the creative meet but do not blend.

2. The Time of Parables

So, what happens when the parable emerges in critical discourse? In the gospels, parables come in clusters or cycles of structurally and thematically related stories, so that each one is, first and foremost, a parable of another parable. Giorgio Agamben writes:

> An implicit link between the structure of parable and the Messianic kingdom is already found in Matthew 13:18–19, where 'the word of the kingdom' (*logos tes basileias*) is what makes it necessary to speak in parables. The parable of the sower explained in this passage treats the logos so that the seed represents language itself (in the exegesis of Mark 4:13, 'He that soweth, soweth the *logos*'). In the series of parables that follow, the messianic kingdom is compared to a field in which good seed and weeds are sown together; to a grain of mustard; to yeast; to treasure hidden in a field; to a merchant in search of a pearl; to a net cast on the water.[16]

As C. H. Dodd has shown, the interpretative gloss on the parable offered in Mark's gospel, and which Agamben alludes to as evidence for his interpretation, is itself inconsistent in that it confuses two divergent ways of reading the parable: it describes the seed as the word, yet the crop is composed of various classes of people. This, Dodd says, draws on two very different sources: the Greek idea of the 'seminal word', and a very similar parable found in the Apocalypse of Ezra that speaks of sowing in relation to people rather than words.[17] Now Agamben's point is that the combination of the kingdom as *logos* and its concomitant annunciation in parables that represent both the kingdom *and each other*, means that the kingdom and its parabolic expression coincide, 'because language itself is what is signified'. But to insist that parables necessarily signify language, is both reductive and at odds with the insights of biblical criticism. Not only so, but Agamben's own account of the parable and its antitype is internally riven by a dependence upon parabolic form that is at odds with the messianic as a move beyond the time and language of parables.

According to Agamben, if parables are to communicate something beyond language, then the very moment of comparison that defines a parable must be 'abolished': the 'as' must become an 'as not'. This is why Paul, the argument goes, never uses parables, but creates a kind of anti-parable in which, rather than comparing similar or dissimilar events, processes or objects, he splits apart identities. Here, Agamben is thinking about that extraordinary passage in 1 Corinthians, chapter 7, that defines 'messianic life' as a denial or reversal of familiar categories of experience and identity:

> But I say this, brethren, the time is short: it remaineth, that both they that have wives be as though they had none; and they that weep, as though they wept not; and they that rejoice, as though they rejoiced not; and they that buy, as though they possessed not; and they that use this world, as not abusing it: for the fashion of this world passeth away. (1 Cor. 7: 29–31)

In this economy, the time of the parable is over, as it related to the 'fashion' of a world that effectively passed away with the resurrection: what remains is messianic time. The kingdom is no longer a matter of self-referential stories that always turn out to be about language: now, what time remains is characterised by a crisis of values, and a form of life that subverts the categories and terminologies of the familiar world. This is the world turned upside down.

What is covered over in this account of the end of the parable, is the fact that it depends upon the emergence of a new parable that is not a story about words alone. Slavoj Žižek, among others, has identified it as 'the parallel between the Christian and the Marxist "messianic" notion of history as the process of the final deliverance of the faithful ones.' [18] Žižek would have us embrace the parable, acknowledge the affinity in order to wrest the Christian heritage away from 'fundamentalist freaks', and in order to defend

human subjectivity against the onslaught of New Age mystagogues whose
vision of cosmic unity veils the threat of a kind of spiritual totalitarianism.
The Christian event, in Žižek's formulation, 'uncouples' us from the kind
of cosmic order that underlies totalitarian systems, because it demands an
individual, personal response to the message of the kingdom rather than an
automatic participation on the basis of our place in the order of things. The
return to parable, then, is a political gesture that confronts Agamben with
an aporia: his overthrowing of the parable has meaning only by virtue of its
participation in a parable – that which draws out the affinity between two
kinds of messianism. His own text actually acknowledges this both in its
structure (six days and a concluding section – paralleling creation) and in
its deployment of a parable from Benjamin's *Theses on the Philosophy of
History*:

> You may recall the image of the hunchback dwarf in Benjamin's first the-
> sis on the philosophy of history – a dwarf is hiding beneath a chessboard
> and, through his movements, assures victory to the mechanical puppet
> dressed in the garb of a Turk. Benjamin borrows this image from Poe;
> however, in transposing this image onto the terrain of the philosophy of
> history, he adds that the dwarf is in fact theology, who 'today, as we know
> is wizened and has to keep out of sight,' and if historical materialism knew
> how to put theology to use, it would win this historical battle thus defeat-
> ing its fearful adversary.[19]

Just as in the gospels, versions of the parable stack up in Agamben's text –
Poe's, Benjamin's, Agamben's. For the latter, of course, the hidden theolo-
gian is Paul – his is the secret operation that 'guides the hands of the puppet
of historical materialism', and thus the parable by which Christian
messianism is a figure for Marxism is interpreted as a history rather than a
fiction. But Agamben's investment in parable returns us to the involutions
of pre-messianic time, to words about words, to stories without end, and to
the problem of what parables are and how they might be read.

On this account, parables, even where their content or deployment is
radical in its alignment with historical materialism, are somewhat conser-
vative: they prevent movement beyond themselves. In a sense this is bound
to be the case inasmuch as we can never dispense with narrative, or trade it
in for something that lies outside of its reach. The messianic, the eschato-
logical, the apocalyptic are always reclaimed by narrative, incorporated as
endings without ends. There is, in this sense, no possibility of narrative
confronting, or yielding to, the 'as not' of messianic time, at least not as
long as we can go on telling stories of messiahs, of apostles, of temporal

crises, or even creating histories of criticism. But this is a paradox since, inherent in the very meaning of narrativity, is the implication that, as Frank Kermode puts it, narratives 'have to mean more, or other, than they manifestly say.'[20]

Parable is, in this sense, the archetypal narrative form. So while narratives keep themselves to themselves in that they refuse to open onto any non-narrative region, possibility, or crisis, they also give way to, or at least invite, interpretative claims. The inexorability of narrative and its parabolic tendency are evident in Agamben's text: it has a kind of narrative shape, progressing through its six days (each chapter is given an ordinal number in relation to a sequence of days over which a seminar is conducted), towards its crisis, turn, or revelation (the concluding section is headed 'Threshold or *Tornada*'). In this sense, the book itself is a parable: a story about time that relates (if only by accident) the moment of messianic crisis to the time of mythic cycles associated with the biblical creation narrative. The emergence of the messianic is a remaking of the world – the dawn of a new time.

But how the function of parables is to be understood is open to interpretation; they either reveal or conceal. The crucial passage, so often turned to by writers on parables, is in Mark's gospel and is part of the interpretation of the parable of the sower:

> Unto you is given to know the mystery of the kingdom of God: but unto them that are without, all these things are done in parables; that they may see, and not perceive; and hearing they may hear, and not understand; lest at any time they should be converted, and their sins should be forgiven them. (Mark 4: 11–12)

C. H. Dodd again:

> According to these verses they [the parables of Jesus] were spoken in order to prevent those who were not predestined to salvation from understanding the teaching of Jesus. This is surely connected with the doctrine of the primitive Church, accepted with modifications by Paul, that the Jewish people to whom Jesus came were by divine providence blinded to the significance of His Coming, in order that the mysterious purpose of God might be fulfilled through their rejection of the Messiah. That is to say, this explanation of the purpose of the parables is an answer to a question which arose after the death of Jesus, and the failure of His followers to win the Jewish people. But that He desired not to be understood by the people in general, and therefore clothed His teaching in unintelligible forms, cannot be made credible on any reasonable reading of the Gospels.[21]

It is curious that this old and vexed issue in biblical criticism, of the nature and purpose of the parables of Jesus, should take us to the heart not only of Agamben's project of elucidating the relevance of the messianic parable in the early years of the twenty-first century, but also into territory explored by that other giant of post-Derridean theory – Žižek. For the distinction that Dodd makes between the teaching of Jesus and its interpretation by the Church is crucial to Žižek's argument for the relevance of that same contemporary parable. He expressly denigrates those who wish to make a distinction between the authentic message of Jesus and the teaching of the Church:

> ... those who acknowledge this direct lineage from Christianity to Marxism, usually fetishise the early 'authentic' followers of Christ against the Church's 'institutionalisation' epitomised by the name of Saint Paul. . . . What these followers of the maxim 'yes to Christ, no to Saint Paul' (who, as was claimed already by Nietzsche, effectively invented Christianity) do is strictly parallel to the stance of those 'humanist Marxists' from the middle of our century whose maxim was 'yes to the early authentic Marx, no to his Leninist ossifying'. And, in both cases, one should insist that such a 'defence' of the 'authentic' is the most perfidious mode of its betrayal: there is no Christ outside Saint Paul.[22]

Once again it is Saint Paul who stands at the crossroads: if, for Agamben, he is the theorist of the messianic, the propounder of, and apologist for, the time that remains, for Žižek, he serves a similar function as the discoverer and interpreter of the 'uncoupling' by means of which the Christian event detaches us from the time of myth, freeing us to become participants in the political age. But, as in Agamben's text, parable persists in Žižek's, not only in that he foregrounds the relationship between Christianity and Marxism, but also in that he draws a 'parallel' between the two waves of fetishising of the 'authentic'.

There is a strange knot here, it seems, forming around the parabolic: to interpret parables as liberating, as tending towards freedom and equality – or at least towards a politics rather than a fixed cosmic order – is to assert the value of an 'authentic' and pre-institutional form of Jesus' teaching, since to accept the institutional framework is to return the parable to its function as exclusionary, elitist or Gnostic encryption implied by the idea of the 'messianic secret'. This is so because, as has been shown, in order to free parable from the taint of the 'messianic secret', Dodd has to distinguish between Jesus' own teaching, and its interpretation by the post-crucifixion church. Yet the interpretation of Christianity as continuous with, or as being in a parabolic relationship with Marxism insists that we cannot divorce the 'authentic' from the 'ossifying' without betraying the liberal force of both. Perhaps the problem here is the sheer ineluctable difficulty that parables always present: they simultaneously reveal and conceal. Although they serve an interpretative purpose, they can never be traded for a certain, fixed, non-narrative meaning, and even though they mean more or other than they manifestly say, they do nothing beside tell simple tales with what Dodd calls 'remarkable realism'. [23] Furthermore, they seem to defy our attempts to identify the very thing that they herald – the messianic. What I mean by this is that if one takes the word of C.H. Dodd, a Bible critic whose work on parables was for many years a standard, one is led to the conclusion that the function of Jesus' parables was a matter of 'realised eschatology' – the announcement that the kingdom of God was already present, that nature and supernature were one and the same, whereas, at least as far as Agamben is concerned, the messianic is marked by the Pauline anti-parable. Highlighting ideological, political, religious, interpretative, theoretical concerns and tying them into a Gordian knot, the parable not only brings to light the problem of the understanding of narrative in general, but also the related problem of criticism at large.

These matters, or something akin to them, were/was long ago brought into the study of literary narrative by Frank Kermode in *The Genesis of Secrecy*. In that book he characterises the reading of the gospels as the paradigm of narrative interpretation precisely because they tell stories that are 'intermittent, forgetful, at times blind or deaf,' that are fraught with 'varying focus, fractured surfaces, over-determinations, displacements.' [24] All narratives share something of this opacity, darkness, or alterity. That is to say that narratives always conceal a layer of meaning, a latent sense that depends upon some kind of 'divinatory' reading: a critical response that delivers a new mode of intelligibility. As Kermode argues, these are the readings we value most highly: those that seem to be the product of some kind of moment of seeing that exceeds the manipulation or deployment of pre-formed theories, techniques, or protocols, and that open up a previously unexplored region of meaning or affect. But however unfamiliar, revelatory or germinal such expositions appear to be, these apparently spontaneous acts of individual genius can, belatedly, be seen to be 'privileged and constrained by the community of the ear'.[25] They derive their value from the institution that recognises, ratifies and celebrates them on the basis of its own interests and procedures. The new is already a return.

But there is another aspect to the secrecy of narratives, one that relates specifically to the function of the parable as Kermode understands it. He derives this understanding from the so-called messianic secret of Mark's gospel (which he takes to be the ur-gospel). The idea here is that the existence of the messianic secret that motivates the telling of parables, means that parables appear to be texts designed to exclude some, but not all, readers / hearers. That this understanding is a problematical one, I have already indicated. Now I want to suggest that it is problematical not only because there may be other ways of approaching the creation and function of parables, but also because the very fact that narratives are perceived to have latent senses means that *each and every reader and hearer* is necessarily an outsider. *There is no inside to the text.* What I mean by this (Kermode himself makes this point) is that the uncovering of the oracular, kerygmatic or spiritual sense, involves the interpreter in a process of selection: the foregrounding or thematising of a limited number of details deemed to be significant for the purpose. For example, in order to make 'The Prodigal Son' a story of repentance and conversion in the Christian mode, the elder brother has to be excised or forgotten; in order to make it a critique of everyday morality, the servants have to be edited out, and so on. But the excision of the elder brother and/or the servants is also a shutting out of the interpreter from those aspects of the story that refuse to yield to the shaping force of the reading. It is not the parable itself that excludes the elder brother or the servants; it is the reading or interpreting that does the shutting out, and it does so at the very point at which that reading attempts to uncover, open out or elucidate the exclusionary meaning.

3. Returning to the Parable

If indeed we are confronted in narratives with texts that have no inside, then we will have remained in the time of parable. We have come to parable anew; we have returned. The return to parable is also the parable of a return: we have left behind the critical turn to language that preoccupied us during the theory years, and returned to the material concerns with which theory was felt to be not inconsistent. But the parable remains, holding us to a freedom that we cannot escape. In certain respects, this makes the parable of the prodigal son our own story. I do not necessarily mean that the prodigal son himself, the boy who runs away and returns, is the critic's only avatar, but that the parable as a whole, including the narrative strands silenced by the religious readings, reflect the critical condition. Which is to say that critical discourse delights in the recovery of the lost, and from this tale of loss and recovery, there are stories to be recovered that cannot be reduced to the familiar religio-moral tale.

You probably know already that story of the runaway boy. You have probably lived it in some way or another: discontent, escape, disillusion-ment, return. For you it might have been home and family – as it was for him – that you needed to leave behind, or it might have been yourself, or religion, or literature, or liberal humanism, or Marxism. It might even have been one of the splendid elaborations of theoretical self-awareness that occu-pied thinkers in the humanities through the 1980s and beyond. Probably it was more than one of the above: there is always something to run away from, even after you have run away.

He has already left home when we first encounter him. And he is already back home. Twice over. The story of the prodigal has something of the char-acter of a myth: its time is cyclical, repetitive, non-specific. For the pattern of escape and return is neither complete nor unidirectional; we can imagine it as having many phases, recurrences and ramifications. Perhaps this is why it occurs not as an isolated tale, but as one parable among three. Two para-bles of the parable lead into the telling of the prodigal's story in Chapter 15 of Luke's Gospel. Parables are told of parables, so that the reference points recede. We know that the boy is lost and recovered before we have even met him, by virtue of the preceding stories on a similar theme. There is a pattern of loss and recovery, or escape and return.

First up is the parable of the lost sheep – the one sheep in a hundred that has strayed from the flock and is out somewhere wandering (like Geoffrey Hartman's critic), in the wilderness. The shepherd seeks him out, picks him up, and carries him home, 'rejoicing.' The soft-hearted sheep man then throws a party for his friends and neighbours to celebrate his recovery of the ovine wanderer.

The second story tells of the lost coin, or silver piece – the one coin in ten that has slipped down the back of the first-century equivalent of a sofa. The woman whose loss this is, lights a candle, sweeps the house and does not stop spring cleaning until the money's found. She too shares the news with her neighbours and invites them to be happy for her.

It is not easy to know if the sheep is an image of the coin or of the boy, or if the coin is an image of both. It is hard to tell the sheep from the groat. Is it the boy who matters, or is it some referent outside of the tales? Or is it the coin? The tripling defers meaning, not only because the images reflect one another, but also because the three-ness of the tale seems self-enclosing in its magical, mystical resonance. The sheep, the coin, and the boy are cognates; they mimic each other just as do the shepherd, the woman and the boy's father and the three sets of vicariously happy neighbours. In each story, loss is turned to gain and the results are published to the joy of (almost) all. You know how it goes.

In the narrative context of Luke's gospel, these stories are cleverly collated to serve as propaganda against the 'Pharisees and scribes' – the usual suspects – carefully gathered not only to hear these stories told against them, but also to provide context and motivation, to prompt the telling by their graceless disparaging of Jesus' consorting with 'publicans and sinners'. Even that opposition is nicely balanced – 'Pharisees and scribes' versus 'publicans and sinners'. The latter become the 'lost ones' in the parables – sheep, coin, son, who have been sought and found; the former are either grumpy neighbours who refuse to rejoice, or the elder brother in the story of the prodigal who carps about the fuss made when his errant brother returns to the fold – chastened, humbled, but ready for a party with dad and the neighbours. Then there is the deliberate staging of the exponential growth of the loss: one in a hundred, one in ten, one in two – one percent, ten percent, fifty percent. This is what will happen to the impatient boy – exponential decline based on multiplying losses: home, money, hope, dignity, in that order. But it will be alright in the end. The loss will be made up and there will be a party.

The collocation of these parables is clearly not innocent; it is very knowing. The composition takes us from sheep to human via the medium of exchange by which people (most of us anyway) relate to sheep – money, preparing us for the motive at the heart of the prodigal's adventure: he wants his share of the wealth and he does not want to wait for the old man to die before he gets it. Money is crucial to these stories not only because it is what the prodigal wants, but also because the parable of the lost coin is the one that links the other two: the sheep and the son have an exchange value because they can be compared to the coin. This, at one level, is what a parable is, of course: a story with an exchange value, albeit a sliding value. Criticism too is an exchange, not only in that it emerges into a marketplace, serves an industry and so on, but also because it involves the textual exchange whereby a set of tropes, meanings, or values pass from the literary work to the critical response and vice versa. I want to cash in my parable at some point, in the interests of material gain; just as I want to trade my reading for a writing.

In this light the tale of the prodigal might be seen as a tale about alienation under the capitalist system: here sentient beings and creative work are reduced to coinage, and the alienation of the prodigal is understandable. Ironically, that would make it a deeply consevative tale: the son returns to the home of his rich father where the servants clothe and feed him, and the system is unaltered by his brief rebellion. But what if the father's house itself were altered by the exchange? In a sense it must be so, although the parable itself is short on detail. The memory of rebellion will never leave; relationships will never be quite the same; they will have changed to some degree, for good or ill. The returned son will have his own memories of wild living, of the proximity of pigs, of hunger, cold, worry, homesickness, of a world beyond the ken of his rooted family; he will always be something of a mystery to them, a bit like the son who turns into an insect in Kafka's famous parable. But they will be a mystery to him too, since he will have missed events, occurrences, conversations that they have shared. Crucially, he will not have shared the anxiety caused by his own absence. And what of that elder son who begrudges his returned sibling the celebration? True, the soppy old dad tries to persuade him to be happy about it on the basis that his inheritance as the firstborn son is secure, but the boy's reaction is not recorded. He might never forgive his errant brother. Some family tension may sow the seed of a future feud, of a revolution. That revolution may already have taken place; if Robbins is right to see in the elder son a figure of the excluded Jew, then the work of Derrida, Bloom, Hartman, Handelman, Boyarin, Bruns, Alter et al, has long since turned upside down the world of critical exchange.

Like parable, criticism is always exchange, both because it involves dialogue and because it transports meanings between the creative, cultural or literary text and the analytical discourse: it trades its reading for writing. It is also economic in that it operates as such an exchange, and in that in that it carries its texts to market. Furthermore, its procedures always inolve a kind of expenditure: that which is reaped or gleaned and garnered from earlier work is put together with the intellectual resources of the critic, and then expended: facts, ideas, observations and arguments are used up on and in the new work. In that the critic reaps no reward (by which I do not mean that most academic publications are unpaid, and that returns from academic books are usually negligible, but that the written is always lost to its author: it spells the author's diasappearance, their death, as Barthes put it), this is not investment; it is what Robbins calls 'the prodigal's uncalculating expenditure'. [26] Criticism, as exchange, is, therefore, always implicated in parables. Parables count upon the currency of narrative images, and often turn currency itself into their central image of human relations. There is a persistent economic strand to the stories of the prodigal, the lost sheep and the lost coin, as there is to just about all of Jesus' reputed oeuvre – the parables concern such things as the earning of livings (fishing and farming), and the finding of treasure and rare pearls. In many parables, religious defection is encoded as financial loss, and the parable that follows the prodigal's tale picks up and accentuates this very theme.

It matters a great deal what follows, and how following is understood. Following is not straightforward, for it is part of the frame in which a thing appears. Frame up to frame. The parable of the prodigal son is framed by the stories that precede and succeed it in Luke's Gospel; it also serves as part of the frame for those other pieces that surround it.

What *does* follow the prodigal? A problematical and much debated story of financial (mis)management. It involves a rich man and his steward. The steward, accused of wasting his master's money, is sacked on the spot. Since he doesn't fancy a life of hard labour, he gathers his master's debtors and halves their debts. The rich man sees that his quick-thinking former employee has re-couped at least some of what would otherwise have to be written off as a bad debt, and gives him back his job. At least, I think that is what happens; it is not very clear. The interpretative spin put on it by Luke's Jesus is somewhat ambiguous too: 'And I say unto you, Make to yourselves friends of the mammon of unrighteousness; that when ye fail, they may receive you into everlasting habitations' (Luke 16:9). That may mean something like: be nice to people you meet on the way up as you are sure to run into them again on the way down. Or it may mean: plan for failure. Or perhaps the implication is that God favours those who know the importance of buying good friends. Whatever the case, the story's focus is economic. It is about relations of production. Money is a metaphor for the soul, just as the spiritual message of Christian messianism becomes a metaphor for historical materialism. That is what parable means.

Christian messianism and historical materialism coalesce in the way the parable of the prodigal son deals with servants. Unnamed and unnumbered, they nonetheless play certain pivotal roles in the story. We hear of them first when, at his lowest ebb, the runaway son's thoughts turn to what he has lost: 'When he came to himself, he said, How many hired servants of my father's have bread enough and to spare, and I perish with hunger? I will arise and go to my father' (Luke 15: 17–18). The prodigal's inner dialogue posits his own superiority over the servants as a reason to return. Why should the servants have food to spare, and he no food at all? It is in the memory of his forsaken position in the hierarchy that his penitence lies – he is motivated by self-pity, focused in his reduction to a status below that of one of his father's staff members. First and foremost, he has betrayed an economy that is inextricable from the father–son relationship: he characterises his return to the system as a return to the father.

Implicit in such a thought is the conviction that his current state of affairs is an inversion of economic order, and his intention to return is characterised as an acknowledgement of that inversion: 'I will arise and go to my father, and will say unto him, Father, I have sinned against heaven, and before thee, And am no more worthy to be called thy son: make me as one of thy hired servants' (Luke 15: 18–19). Here, the hierarchy is made manifest: he is not worthy to be a son, but he *is* worthy to be a servant. So, while

Harrison may be right to characterise the parable as espousing values that are at odds with the 'underlying structures of social practices and their corresponding systems of concepts,' it is so only within the limits of the established economy. Which means that if, as already suggested, the story of the prodigal son is framed in Luke's gospel as a response to a social judgement about the worth of 'publicans and sinners', it apparently has nothing to say about the comparative worth of servants: it leaves the hierarchy and its implicit values quite intact.

It is clear here that the effect of narrative is beyond the control of any argument because it does not fall within the ambit of any conceptualisation or categorically state-able problematic. What I mean by this is that an argument based on the relationship between father and son will tend to take us in one direction (say, the liberal reading proposed by Harrison), that is undermined by the reading that I have just offered – one that takes as its central concern the economic and political implications of the story: exchange value and the position of the servants. Furthermore, as the confrontation between the interpretations of parable in Agamben and Žižek showed, the politicising of the story in terms of economic power structures, rather than issuing in a coherent, recoverable critique of capitalist mores, muddies the waters, working against that which seeks to make of it a radical and power-resistant intervention. Similarly, because the story is just that, a story, other lines of force will also cross through it: the story of the elder brother as pursued by Robbins, for example.

In this light, we might also want to ask about the boy's mother. The story is silent about her, and this too is a parable: the absence of women from, or their obscuration within, the systems of economic exchange has long been a defining characteristic of capitalist culture. The mother's feelings about her son's disappearance are not recorded. Her joy on his return is not mentioned. Another seed of discontent? Another latent revolution? Another revolution that is already underway?

Some of these figures are outsiders, players of bit parts, or of no part at all. Figures of the Jew, of women, of the exploited or enslaved, they are also, as Kermode's work shows us, figures of the critic. Parables make such roles both possible and inevitable, because the parable, as a bearer of messianic meaning, creates a cultural outside, and because it remains irreducibly narrative – a discursive space irreducible to any critical mapping: a form which both invites and excludes us without limit.

The Dwarf

The story is told of an automaton constructed in such a way that it could play a winning game of chess, answering each move of an opponent with a countermove. A puppet in Turkish attire and with a hookah in its mouth sat before a chessboard placed on a large table. A system of mirrors created the illusion that this table was transparent from all sides. Actually, a little hunchback who was an expert chess player sat inside and guided the puppet's hands by means of strings. One can imagine a philosophical counterpart to this device. The puppet called 'historical materialism' is to win all the time. It can easily be a match for anyone if it enlists the services of theology, which today, as we know, is wizened and has to keep out of sight.[1]

In order to get over the wall, it is sometimes necessary to get into a basket. The freedom to be what we are may be defined by the means of escape we employ. Sometimes I think that I am defined by the act of confining myself in this curious box, behind a system of mirrors. I am this box rather than what the mirrors show. I have lost track of the years since I first found myself here – the ghost in the machine. I think I will always have been here. So much time, all of it confined to this little ark in the light and shade diffused through a translucent chequerboard ceiling.

I have thought of escape, but that was what put me here in the first place. A kind of secession or withdrawal. I felt my world diminishing, and moved to set up my own constraints, a structure of my own devising. No-one put me here, you understand. I am not a captive. I drew some lines, that's all. Call it asceticism. Anyway, I cannot be sure that by now there is anything out there to escape to, anything that I would recognise, that is, nor anyone who might recognise me. Memory is the problem: remembering and being remembered. Next game.

The important thing is to be thinking ahead; at least three moves. But thinking ahead is also thinking back; to imagine what will be by remembering what has passed. History is a function of the visionary. The black squares and the white squares. Makes no sense otherwise. I think this is what they mean by eternity. Neither one thing nor the other. Always both. That makes keeping track of the time almost impossible. It is always both day and night; never one thing or the other; always both. I gave up trying to understand the pattern long ago; or was it yesterday?

There have been so many incarnations, every one the same. Similar, anyway. I say 'incarnations'; it might be the wrong word for this kind of embodiment. I have always been unsure about flesh. It hurts to be in here, I can tell you. The weakness of the flesh has cost me a few games. More and more as I get older. Try again.

Inside this box of mirrors, their backs all turned to me, there is no reflective surface around me in which I might see my image. The darkened glass of my own mind is not enough. It has no ground but its own taint. Not that I mind, you understand; I have never been especially vain. I hear that I am old and wrinkled. I must be. I think I was born that way. I was certainly never very lovely, though there were admirers in the old days; mostly men; men of a certain disposition. I never loved, never understood love as anything but a concept. The theory always attracted me: I like the idea and have been known to discourse upon it. But who would love a thing like me – a functionary, a fairground attraction, a deformed little organ-grinder? From time to time, I have even heard voices that claim I am dead. Played a couple of them off the board – just by surviving, just by being here and playing the game. They didn't expect that. I've lost a few too. It took some getting used to, losing after a thousand years of winning every time. Hell of a thing. Scary as hell. It was like the end of the world. End of the bloody world. Maybe it was actually the end of the world as it had been. Maybe this is simply another world – something just flipped over and there it is. Who would know? It is certainly true that I am not what I was; I am no longer the central attraction in this fairground full of grotesques, shysters, and white-knuckle rides. Not many want to play my game now, and this makes me wonder if those who speak of my death may not be right. I have no way of knowing whether this is life or death. Life and death, I suppose. The black squares and the white. Who would know? Next game.

I live mostly in memory, like most old people. But that is what makes the future possible: reliving the great moments that are yet to come. I go over and over the same old things. No, that's not quite right. I return to things, but I do not find them the same as they were. Memory is like that, isn't it. It'll be the death of me. If I'm still alive, that is. But, true or not (both true and untrue, maybe), I have my favourite memories. Old Blougram, now, he was a player. Such finesse. Never stopped talking the whole game through. The rhetoric would break the heart of any honest person. Break your heart if you'd any principles at all. I admit, with some shame, that he learned all he knew from me, but in the end he was just too good; got the better of me. The pupil always surpasses the master. Every pupil stands on the shoulders of a giant. Or a midget. No-one is content with what they learn. He stood on me alright. Stood on me with all his ecclesiastical weight – heavy as a thousand tomes. His trick was to play the game by his own rules. I mean, he could reinterpret the board itself; where you saw black, he said he saw white. Not only that, but he also insisted that you'd been playing by his rules all along, otherwise there could have been no game. Would that matter? Play on; that's the safest thing. Play on.

I've had to change, to adapt in order to survive. To evolve, you might say. Yes, I've heard of Darwin. He wasn't much of player himself. That's why he was so dangerous. You can only make your move against people who play; if they don't play, you're lost. I often think that he was the first – the first real non-player. Strange though, because although Mr Darwin rarely visited me, he came just often enough for his followers to think that he had a stake in the game. I was lucky there, I think. Well, I used to think so. It took a while for me to realise that he was actually stealing the pieces from the board: took the white king, I believe, and pocketed three of the bishops. Nothing's been the same since. It's hard to play without those pieces. Different game altogether. I've had to adapt. I keep on adapting. New incarnations. New strategies. Next game.

I have heard that there is a replica of me in a museum somewhere, life-like in every detail. It moves, they say, by virtue of some kind of mechanism that wears out and has to be replaced after about ten years of constant playing. I have heard talk of it so often. They say that it is so similar to me that it is even capable of making the same moves, of replicating my stratagems, and repeating the syntax of my play. Some say it could beat me in a fair game. What would a fair game be? I am the unfairness of the game, the concealed advantage, the unknown quantity. But what might be concealed behind the mirrors of my replicant? Unless you can get behind the mirror, you never know what you're up against. You might just be up against yourself. Ah. Now I begin to wonder which is the original and which is the copy. Am I a replicant? How do I know that I am not the copy? Only my memories. Can they have been forged? Stalemate. New game.

These days I live on memories. Did I say that before? It is just as well that memories change, or I'd be like some brainless little goldfish, swimming around and around in the same little bowl, in the same few inches of water, drifting over the same few pebbles and plastic weed, forever rotting, but never passing away. I used to think that the past was set in stone, that it was unchangeable, that it followed you around like a tin can tied to your ankle, embarrassing you more with every new day. But I have discovered that the past is as open as the future. More open in fact, because you can't change what you don't yet know. To relive the games of the past is also to rewrite them with hindsight, to uncover in them the possibilities that were covered over close up, that emerge only in long perspective. I like to return to the new, to go back and listen again to the unsung song, to plot the unmade moves and imagine the universes germinating in each latent game, picture worlds piling up like grains of rice, their number doubling on each successive square.

I often wonder if I could have been other than I am. Or if there are other versions of me, piled up like grains of rice on the squares of some bigger board than this. Who would know?

Your move. I think.

Keywords
The Prodigal Daughter

1. Finding Keys

There was a time when some kind of an escape seemed necessary in order to write at all. I do not mean that pressure of work, or family commitments, or the shackles of institutional bureaucracy were so demanding or oppressive that one simply had to head for the hills in order to find some peace and quiet. I refer to the fact that language itself had taken on a carceral aspect that seemed to make writing, at worst impossible, at best a self-reflexive activity in thrall to the perception that all language could do was refer to itself. That theories of textuality gave rise to the sense of language as a form of imprisonment was evident, in those days, in a variety of titles and slogans in critical discourse: Fredric Jameson gave us 'the prison-house of language', Lacan made us 'hostages of the word', Derrida told us that there was '*no outside* to the text', and then, latterly, Valentine Cunningham invited us into the 'reading gaol'; we were bound in 'chains of signification', and (some of us) found ourselves in pursuit of 'hermeneutic keys'.

The story of the prodigal taking leave of his stifling home life seems inviting at such moments: what would be the prodigal response to linguistic internment? It turned out to be the case that, growing tired of repeatedly re-describing the interior of the cell, we conjured it away by means of various tricks. These consisted of: (a) finding reasons to disapprove of the thinkers who put us inside, e.g. having a Nazi past; (b) rediscovering history, i.e. imagining contexts were continuous with, or in a quantifiable relationship with, texts; (c) remembering that Darwin said something about language and evolution, and exploring scientific possibilities for approaching the problem; (d) finding a hole in the ozone layer that (allegedly) was not a text. You can add your own favourite post-theory pastime to the list. These prodigal responses are all of a piece in the sense that they follow the narrative arc of the prodigal himself: they are escape routes. An ill-prepared escape may well lead to repentance and return; I, at least, keep going back. I may be alone. You will know.

What draws me back is the nagging sense that there were always other options that I might have taken, other characters with whom I might have identified, other stories that are yet to be told. I want to go back now, in search of such a story, to remember a figure: that of an excluded sister or daughter who makes her own bid for freedom; we will call her Helen. You will meet her before long, if you do not know her already. To find her, we will need to go back to gaol – back, that is, into Cunningham's reading gaol.

In the Reading Gaol[1] is a book that takes on textualist theories by exploring the ways in which literary texts resist any straightforward or undifferentiated account of language as a mode of imprisonment: they are characterised as insistently opening onto, or drawing into themselves, a real world beyond the confines of closed signifying systems. It is perhaps not surprising then that it is a book that conceals in its pages many keys. In addressing the New Historicism, Cunningham draws our attention to the first bunch: 'To be analytically potent keys, power and desire and bodies and otherness, and all the other going concerns of New Historicists, have to be broken down, particularized, granted the singularity of time and place and person' (46). His point is that such terms are simply items of a newly orthodox jargon, akin to religious language, unless and until they are made to reflect some real-world conditions. Without being pinned down to specific instances or experiences, these buzzwords appear to be little more than gestural. It is a neat trick that allows Cunningham to pull the key into the room, under the door, on a carefully laid bit of fabric: as long as New Historicism views context as no more than another text, it is untrue to, or even blind to, its own best (political) insights. What, we are perhaps led to ask, would be the point of producing critical discourses that draw attention to the construction, uses, or misuses of power, only to then insist that power is merely a textual effect, and those oppressed by it are incapable of resistance since subjectivity is no less a textual effect than is power?

Another way of thinking of this is that the efficacy of the hermeneutic key depends upon the telling of stories: desire, power, otherness etc., only serve a material purpose if they are applied to real lives, if they appear as motivations or drivers of processes within a set of specific and delimited circumstances. Story-telling, narrative, is thus placed at the heart of the critical process: the interaction of word and world depends upon that between the critical and the creative. For, it is the telling of stories that enables the conceptual content of a discourse to find its way into the world beyond the text. Furthermore, the story, inasmuch as it figures an embodying of the concept, is necessarily a parable. A parable is a key story: a story that can be turned about in order to open a world in front of the reader, or turned another way to lock out unwelcome presences.

Cunningham's next key is less obviously related to any specific theoretical formation. He refers to what he calls 'a key moment' in a text by Virginia Woolf (16), and to what he characterises as 'a key chapter' in Paul de Man's *Resistance to Theory* (40). This is a familiar enough gesture in literary criticism: the locating of a textual moment in the light of which the whole piece under consideration can best be understood: the hub of the wheel, the paradigmatic instance, the synecdoche by which the part serves as the whole: the omphalos. This particular key opens the door to psychoanalysis and the work of the two 'Rabbins' encountered in the final chapter of Cunningham's book: Freud and Lacan. The key moment in the dream-text is described by Freud in *The Interpretation of Dreams* as the dark navel. Considering this, as part of his essay on dictionaries, Cunningham shows how Samuel Weber's attempt to define the origin of the dream by pursuing dictionary definitions, inevitably leads him in a circle, as definition leads to definition (156–8).

Literary criticism that attempts to turn the key moment into its hermeneutic entrée, runs the same risk when it tries to uncover the navel of the text, since every text opens onto, leads back to, and feeds off, other texts. A text is polyumbilicate: the centre, once located, always reappears elsewhere. Textual energies seem to flow without source or estuary, like the waterfall in Escher's famous drawing. And yet, maybe there is a secret source hidden beneath the (non)ground of the (post)modern landscape. For Cunningham, anyway, the spring is biblical. His final chapter assiduously seeks out the repressed Biblicism in the work of major theorists like Barthes, Derrida, Bloom, Hartman and Lacan. The latter reads the navel of the dream 'as a place of would-be oblivion, of the non-, or un-, a lack or gap . . .' marking the repressed presence of nothing less than God' (379). Thus Nietzsche's myth of the death of God can be seen as a belated explanation of the navel scar. Since the presence or absence of God, or the existence of a transcendental signified, or the recoverability of the truth of the text is at stake here, it is possible that we are confronted with a choice of reading: does the world disappear into a textual void, an abyss of self-reference? Or is this seeming emptiness simply a God-shaped hole at the centre of (post)modern interpretation – a hole that marks the absence of a faith that might fill it? Is the theoretical a wilful repression of a necessary and inescapable logocentrism, or is it a potentially joyous playfulness characteristic of the post-christian, postmodern condition? There was a time when I would have argued, when I did argue, the case for the former proposition. But I fled my father's house (he was an evangelical Christian and a Baptist minister), and now inhabit the space between such possibilities, eking out a precarious, agnostic, prodigal existence in the wilderness. From here I see that the question leads to another of Cunningham's keys.

In the Reading Gaol goes to great lengths to establish the presence of the world in the text. In a doubled text from Virginia Woolf's diary, and from her letters, Cunningham finds the world encroaching upon 'this little narrative – at once so strikingly a writing, about text . . . but also so emphatically about the knowable, touchable world of city streets, shops, country houses, possessions, persons who exist outside the narrative' (10–11). 'And the key word,' he tells us, 'is *also*'. The also-worldness of texts turns up again and again throughout the book in many guises. It is present in its most abstract form as the 'intermediate nature of signs and texts, poised between reference inwards and outwards, always stuck with and between words and the world' (93–4). Hardy's detailed historical research forms a more concrete example of the world impinging upon the text, as do the bodies of maimed workers in the Dickensian industrial hard times. Then there is the curious appearance of the Huntley and Palmers biscuit tin in *Heart of Darkness*. Like all keys, the *also* works both ways: it denies legitimacy to the idea that we can choose the world and dispense with the text, but it also insists that we cannot yield to an absolute textuality that refers only to itself. That is to say, alongside the also-worldness of the text, Cunningham is keen to show us the also-textuality of the world, again in many guises: the reciprocal (at times undecidable) relationship between parasite and host; the enigmatic character of texts; the post-Babel confusion of tongues; the Bible-dependence of our interpretative practices.

Bible-dependence helps us to locate the next key. The Bible, the Great Code of Art, as Blake called it and as Northrop Frye duly expounded it, might also be the ur-text of theory. Cunningham describes what he sees as the covert Biblicism of the modern theorist-cabbalists as 'the big ideological key to (post)modernist critical theory and writing practice' (393). The evidence that he adduces in the final chapter of the book is certainly impressive. The ingenious repressions by means of which the Bible's ubiquitous influence is translated out of texts by Rousseau, Kafka, Freud and so on, are (equally ingeniously) uncovered, to show that '(post)modernism's blasphematory wrestle with the biblical' is actually a 'struggle to silence, nullify, annihilate the prime father and his textual fathering. The repressions are, occasionally admitted to. Often they're hotly denied – are repressed, in fact' (378).

The return of this repressed aligns itself with the return of the repressed presence of the world in the text, and with the concomitant return of an insistent and indefeasible textuality, as detailed in the long triptych that forms Cunningham's central chapter.

On this account, the Bible (in its character of hermeneutic key), is a privileged analogue (a favourite parable, maybe) of both language and the world. From Babel to Pentecost, and from the deadly sociolinguistics of the shibboleth (Judges 12), to the psycholinguistics of worship (1 Corinthians 14), the Bible certainly has a great deal to say about language. It also has much to say about the world, and the history of its interpretation, which has often been a matter of life and death, a matter of imprisonment, torture, and even of war, leaves us in no doubt that words and the world are never closed off from one another. But, of course, something has been passed over silently in this act of mediation between language and reality. It is this: the Bible is a text, or a set of texts; it is not a sign. It is not (primarily) even a collection or combination of signs. Principally it tells stories, and something happens between the level of the semiotic and the level of the text (on which the stories take shape), for which Cunningham has not accounted.

2. Turning

I am not satisfied with this account of theory, nor with Cunningham's resistance to it. It is an appealing picture, I grant you, but it is not satisfying because so much is left undone, and it is precisely this that calls me back now, today, a decade later. I want to believe in Cunningham's theology of reciprocation. I like the symmetry of it, the cool interdependence of text and world. What troubles me is that I do not find real, flesh-and-blood bodies, maimed or otherwise, in texts; nor do I find biscuit tins clattering about between the pages. In other words, something is missing: a story, or an argument, that might help us to connect words with the world so that we might go home and write in peace. Firstly I shall look for the argument, then I shall tell you the story; that is when we shall meet Helen.

In order to make the *also-worldness* pole of his formulation work, Cunningham has to escape the trap of post-Saussurean formalism. In the first chapter of *In the Reading Gaol*, he seems to read deconstruction as a continuation of the Saussurean insistence on the arbitrariness of the linguistic sign, and points to what he sees as Emile Benveniste's proof of the falsity of this notion. Despite this, he goes on to align himself with Derrida's famous formulation of the two interpretations of interpretation – the search for truth or origin, as against Nietzschean suspicion – and with Derrida's insistence that there is no question of choosing between them.[2] At the theoretical level, the power not to choose is produced by the 'intermediate nature of signs and texts, poised between reference inwards and outwards, always stuck with and between words and the world.' If this is really the case, then the subject of language is similarly 'stuck', unable to choose (or to move) between the self-reference of language and its worldliness. But this presupposes that signs and texts share a nature; manifestly, they do not. The sign is the product of a belated analysis of language, of text; it is the device or contrivance of an approach that seeks to objectify language for the sake of (scientific) study. Furthermore, the deconstruction of the sign depends not upon its arbitrariness, but upon its structure. The two faces of the sign -the signified and the signifier (or the concept and the sound-image), form a structure that, as Derrida demonstrated on *Of Grammatology,* is unstable, self-defeating, and that cannot hold.

On the other hand, in works such as *The Conflict of Interpretations, Hermeneutics and the Human Sciences,* and *The Rule of Metaphor,* Paul Ricoeur has shown that meaning is not primarily semiotic; rather it is primarily semantic; that is to say, it is produced not at the level of the sign, but at the level of the sentence and the text. On this account, it is the *text* that is positioned between the word and the world, while the sign comes to light only by means of the suspension of the work of the text in a moment of analytic regression. Language use subtends the appearance of the sign, both logically and chronologically: a sign can serve as a sign only if it first appears in a text that underwrites its semiotic function: there is no such thing as a sign in the singular; there are signs only when and where there is syntax. Signs and texts cannot both occupy a mediatory position between words and the world, as Cunningham claims, since words *are* linguistic signs; they cannot come between themselves and something else. There can be mediation of this kind only if signs and texts do not share a nature, if, in fact, the text transcends the order of the sign in order to reach the world. Or, more accurately: *the world reaches us in texts,* and we break them into signs. We dissect the flow. Language is no more a system of signs than water is a system of molecules. Once this has been understood, the doubleness of interpretation – its division between limitless suspicion and truth-seeking inquiry – seems somewhat less convincing. What I mean is that if it is *the critique of the sign* that opens before us the Nietzschean option, then suspicion is not, in fact, limitless; it is confined to the truth-telling status of *analysis* rather than being applicable to the work of language as a whole. This does not imply that synthesis and analysis are in a dialectical relationship, but that 'synthesis' is nothing other than the flow of language prior to analysis; synthesis is made visible only by the counter movement of analysis.

This has important ramifications for analytical discourse, not least for the kind of analysis practiced by literary critics. The act or performance of analysis cuts back the text to the elements of a structure, whatever the theoretical (or even the untheorised) approach adopted, since it seeks escape from repetition of the text by means of a breaking into – or a breaking up of – the text, according to its own needs and desires. The interpreter inevitably performs what Kermode calls 'a grandiose neglect of portions of the text,' to the extent that 'it appears that the history of interpretation may be thought as a history of exclusions, which enable us to seize upon this issue rather than on some other as central, and choose from the remaining mass only what seems most compliant.'[3] Criticism necessarily homes in on its selected detail, bracketing all that is not germane within its purview, so that the work of the text, as text, is suspended. Indefinitely. This can never be undone by or within the critical performance, since to pass from the whole to the part is to shift between orders of representation that are strictly incommensurable. Once the order of the text is left behind (as it necessarily is in every analytical gesture), the system closes language in upon itself, chains it up in signifiers without signifieds, shutting out the world. In order to escape this enclosure we need to tell stories that are also acts of criticism. A story that is also an act of criticism – this is what parable means.

3. The Story

What story shall we tell that might help us? What story addresses the reciprocal lockings in and out of language and the world? What story might be told of an escape that is not *from* language, but *into* language? The life of Helen Keller, who found language by means of physical contact with the world, with water running over her skin – 'the wonderful cool something' that flowed over her hand, while the letters w-a-t-e-r were traced in her palm, demonstrates the contact, not of signs and things, words and objects, but of thought with an experiential syntax: the flow of the world and the stream of unbroken language. Her remarkable book *The Story of My Life,* in which the encounter between language and the world is narrated, has a good deal to tell us that neither theory nor the resistance to theory can say.[4] I will, of course, have to break into, or break up, the lovely flow of Helen's story. This is heartbreaking, but what can I do? I will not be able to touch your skin with my words, nor pour water through these pages for you. I am stuck in this text. I am sorry. Try to forgive me. Maybe something will happen to change things before the end of the book.

One thing that makes this story particularly potent in this context, is that it inverts the premise of the reading gaol, or of those discourses that have turned language into a species of confinement. Helen Keller, by her own testimony, perceived her disabilities as a non-reading gaol: 'A few impressions stand out vividly from the first years of my life; but "the shadows of the prison-house" are on the rest' (13). She speaks of Anne Sullivan, the woman who brought her to language, as 'my teacher – who was to set my spirit free' (17). Again, she describes her lack of language as 'invisible hands' holding her, and she adds: 'I made frantic efforts to free myself' (23). Elsewhere, she refers to 'the prison of silence' (55), and to 'life's shut gate' (110); together such references link into a chain of metaphors that suggests her exclusion from language is perceived as a confinement.

Having lost both her sight and her hearing as a result of an illness while still a very young child, Keller writes of her struggle to attain linguistic competence, to read, to write, and to speak, and eventually to complete a university education, as a process of breaking out, of escaping *into* language. While some theorists bemoan, and others celebrate, what Robert Graves called the 'cool web of language' that 'winds us in', Keller depicts her struggle to escape from the prison-house of non-language. Her aphasia is the return of the repressed: a life that disrupts the theories of textuality by re-posing the question of language and freedom from the other side of the prison door. She can be seen, in this sense, as one of the characters whose role in a story has been forgotten, occulted, or at least played down. Perhaps we owe it to her to let her tell some of the story for herself here: that part of it that is concerned with her release.

The morning after my teacher came she led me into her room and gave me a doll. The little blind children at the Perkins Institution had sent it and Laura Bridgman had dressed it; but I did not know that until afterwards. When I had played with it a little while, Miss Sullivan slowly spelled into my hand the word 'd-o-l-l.' I was at once interested in this finger play and tried to imitate it. When I finally succeeded in making the letters correctly I was flushed with childish pleasure and pride. Running downstairs to my mother, I held up my hand and made the letters for doll. I did not know that I was spelling a word or even that words existed; I was simply making my fingers go in monkey-like imitation. In the days that followed I learned to spell in this uncomprehending way a great many words, among them *pin*, *hat*, *cup* and a few verbs like *sit*, *stand* and *walk*. But my teacher had been with me several weeks before I understood that everything has a name.

One day, while I was playing with my new doll, Miss Sullivan put my big rag doll into my lap also, spelled 'd-o-l-l' and tried to make me understand that 'd-o-l-l' applied to both. Earlier in the day we had had a tussle over the words 'm-u-g' and 'w-a-t-e-r'. Miss Sullivan had tried to impress it upon me that 'm-u-g' is *mug* and that 'w-a-t-e-r' is *water*, but I persisted in confounding the two. In despair she had dropped the subject for the time, only to renew it at the first opportunity. I became impatient at her repeated attempts and, seizing the new doll, I dashed it upon the floor. I was keenly delighted when I felt the fragments of the broken doll at my feet. Neither sorrow or regret followed my passionate outburst. I had not loved the doll. In the still, dark world in which I lived there was no strong sentiment or tenderness. I felt my teacher sweep the fragments to one side of the hearth, and I had a sense of satisfaction that the cause of my discomfort was removed. She brought me my hat, and I knew I was going out into the warm sunshine. This thought, if a wordless sensation may be called a thought, made me hop and skip with pleasure.

We walked down the path to the well-house, attracted by the fragrance of the honeysuckle with which it was covered. Someone was drawing water, and my teacher placed my hand under the spout. As the cool stream gushed over one hand she spelled into the other the word *water*, first slowly, then rapidly. I stood still, my whole attention fixed upon the motions of her fingers. Suddenly I felt a misty consciousness as of something forgotten – a thrill of returning thought; and somehow the mystery of language was revealed to me. I knew then that 'w-a-t-e-r' meant the wonderful cool something that was flowing over my hand. That living word awakened my soul, gave it light, hope, joy, set it free! There were barriers still, it is true, but barriers that could in time be swept away.

I left the well-house eager to learn. Everything had a name, and each name gave birth to a new thought. As we returned to the house every object which I touched seemed to quiver with life. That was because I saw everything with the strange, new sight that had come to me. On entering the door I remembered the doll I had broken. I felt my way to the hearth and picked up the pieces. I tried vainly to put them together. Then my eyes filled with tears; for I realized what I had done, and for the first time I felt repentance and sorrow. (27–29)

This moment of escape, repentance, conversion, new sight, that is also the entry into language, is, recognisably, a version of the prodigal; yet is also a re-writing. Here escape does not precede repentance and return; rather escape *is* return, rediscovery, rebirth; repentance *follows*. There is always another story, a different sequence, an alternative construction of what follows (from) what. Here, escape is a return to language: the 'strange, *new* sight', is also 'a thrill of *returning* thought'. Language does not arrive as a chain of signification, but as a cool flowing of the world over the skin that brings to light a continuity between world, body, mind and language. It is a new continuation of an unknown familiar: a following that does not follow.

4. The Story within the Story

It would be a happy moment to leave the story. But just when you think language and the world are playing together nicely, textuality returns to disrupt the game. The border between word and world, between life and letter, runs through the Keller autobiography. It can be seen in the book-ishness of its subject as she turns again and again to the books that fill her memory, that are part of this story of her life, and it can traced meandering through the quotations from poems and the allusions to the Bible that punctuate the text. But it appears most clearly in the admission that she believes her consciousness to be excessively fraught with assimilated texts. At the commencement of chapter XXI, she opens the question of the significance of books to her self-formation:

> I have thus far sketched the events of my life, but I have not shown how much I have depended on books not only for pleasure and for the wisdom they bring to all who read, but also for that knowledge which comes to others through their eyes and their ears. Indeed, books have meant so much more in my education than in that of others, that I shall go back to the time when I began to read. (89–90)

Here, the dependence upon books not only forms the consciousness of the writer, but also works to shape the narrative in which that consciousness is represented, and, once again, it involves a return, a going back, a recapitulation. Language, whether written or spoken, seems to be a return, even when it first arrives; it is always a going back; necessarily, in a sense, since language has always already arrived before the subject.

In one particularly striking episode, Keller's story highlights the inter-weaving of life and literature in a way that has a profound impact upon her subjectivity, and subjects the creative mode to a painful interrogation by the critical.

Key moment

Permit me to introduce a neologism here. At least, it may be a neolo-gism, or it may follow certain other uses. It is difficult to be sure which words are one's own, and which have already been claimed. This is precisely the problem that Helen Keller's story foregrounds, and the word I need is itself a key term that expresses the dilemma: *anagnosis*. I have cut it on the model of *anamnesis,* to suggest the uncovering of knowledge in the human sciences by means of genealogy, etymology or archaeology (as, for example, in Nietzsche's *The Genealogy of Morals,* or Foucault's *The Archaeology of Knowledge*). I am aware of the irony involved in proposing a Platonic recovery of lost knowledge as a model for the Nietzschean / Foucauldian project of dissolving origins in a play of differences, of replacing the ground of knowledge with a 'tropological space', but the choice of a backward-looking epistemology signalled by the terms 'genealogy' and 'archaeology', seems to me to make those terms and the discourses constructed under their signs, anti-cognitive versions of anamnesis. They may seek a kind of anti-knowledge, but they attempt to recognise (to *return* to cognition) knowledge's non-origin, and to do so by unearthing the secret history covered over by the metaphors of metaphysics. Now I have cut the key, I will proceed with it in my pocket.

In 1892, we are told, the young, book-obsessed Helen was profoundly disturbed by a set of circumstances that arose as a result of her writing 'a little story called "The Frost King"'. The effect of the episode was such, Keller says, that 'Books lost their charm for me' (58). She had written the story for a man who had befriended her at the Perkins Institution for the Blind during the autumn after she had learned to speak. The recipient of the story was 'delighted' with it and 'published it in one of the Perkins Institution reports.' Soon after publication, Keller observes, it was discovered that a similar story 'called "The Frost Fairies" by Miss Margaret T. Canby, had appeared before I was born in a book called "Birdie and His Friends". The two stories were so much alike in thought and language that it was evident Miss Canby's story had been read to me, and that mine was a plagiarism' (59). This realisation caused Helen astonishment and grief. It was not, on her account, a deliberate attempt to pass off someone else's work as her own. As far as Helen was concerned the story *was* her own.

Grief seems to be the appropriate emotion. This is a kind of death. To find that a story that is your own – 'it is my story' (59), Helen insists – is also someone else's story, is un-selving, soul destroying. Her own imagination now appeared to be shot-through with the language of others, constituted by reading rather than by self-creation:

> . . . how could it possibly have happened? I racked my brain until I was weary to recall anything about the frost that I had read before I wrote 'The Frost King'; but I could remember nothing, except the common reference to Jack Frost, and a poem for children, 'The Freaks of the Frost', and I knew I had not used that in my composition. (59)

How could life and text become so confused? How can a self and a story from outside it become so entangled? The very life that questions the postmodern condition as imprisonment within language, lends support to its suspicion of the autonomous subject, and enhances its celebration of intertextuality and intersubjectivity. Not only was the child, Helen, distressed by the issue, but Keller, the autobiographer, is still not free from a Bloomian 'anxiety of influence':

> Everything I found in books that pleased me I retained in my memory, consciously or unconsciously, and adapted it. The young writer, as Stevenson has said, instinctively tries to copy whatever seems most admirable, and he shifts his admiration with astonishing versatility. It is only after years of this sort of practice that even great men have learned to marshal the legion of words which come thronging through every byway of the mind.
>
> I am afraid I have not yet completed this process. It is certain that I cannot always distinguish my own thoughts from those I read, because what I read becomes the very substance and texture of my mind. Consequently, in nearly all that I write, I produce something which very much resembles the crazy patchwork I used to make when I first learned to sew. (63)

The text is also the texture of the mind, and it is replicated in the patchwork textile of more writing.

The patchwork condition of the writer's mind was brought to book only by means of a painful *anagnosis:* the recovery of a lost or repressed knowledge. Helen had to be convinced of the story's external source: 'It was difficult,' she writes, 'to make me understand this; but when I did understand I was astonished and grieved' (59). The writer was forced to recognise or to remember her own secondariness – the prior claim of another author upon her own words. Somehow, she had lost the knowledge of the story's exteriority, and only an external pressure could bring about the *anagnosis* by which another's words could be known to be such. All her self-questioning could not produce the relevant memory. But the incident delivered a salutary, if poignant, lesson in textuality: 'So this sad experience may have done me good and set me thinking on some of the problems of composition' (63). The critical moment – the judgement that intervenes between what an author knows of their own text, and what appears in the world under the prodigal sign of the author, at first appears lethal: as all poststructuralists know, it kills the author. But it also returns the author to herself, to the *creative* judgement that is a chastened or penitent self-reflection informed by the alienating echoes that reshape her own voice in her ears. In this strange form, the world arrives with language.

There is loss and gain here. The lesson is learned, but a friend is lost: 'My only regret is that it resulted in the loss of one of my dearest friends . . . ' (64). Who was this lost friend? The man at the Perkins Institution for the Blind, for whom the story had been written, and for whom one was either an author or a cheat. He could not believe in Helen's loss of herself, nor in her experience of *anagnosis*; he could not accept the lost autonomy of the authorial subject. Ironically, he was called Mr Anagnos.

5. The Cure for Graphosclerosis

Helen's anxiety would not go away. Writing is an anxious business; there is much to be anxious about: influence, ignorance, indolence; not to mention the things that do not get done during the process: the living excluded by writing. Then there is the loss of self: the death one suffers in authorship, both because control over meaning is ceded, and because to write is to become the crossing point between one self and another: a junction of words that one can never fully possess, that have belonged to another, and will do so again. But, when writing threatens the self, the self fights back in seizures of the hand that prevent writing. Keller recalls that she would be gripped by a sense of existential doubt, a fear that her words were not her own; then, expressing an idea she would spell into her teacher's hand: 'I am not sure it is mine' (66). Such doubts would lead to what can only be called graphosclerosis: ' . . . in the midst of a paragraph I was writing, I said to myself, "Suppose it should be found that all this was written by some one long ago!" An impish fear clutched my hand, so that I could not write any more that day. And even now I sometimes feel the same uneasiness and disquietude' (66). *I sometimes feel the same uneasiness and disquietude. Even now. Maybe these words are not my own.*

The writing of this very life is at stake here – it has been repressed by the text of another author that seems to spring up in the place of creative thought. How, then, did this text, this story of a life, come to be written? It began with a 'prophetic vision' that overcame the anxiety of *anagnosis*. Anne Sullivan, Helen's teacher, persuaded her twelve-year-old charge to begin a brief account of her life, as a means of restoring her self-confidence. The threat of textuality requires the reassertion of life. In an illustration of what Paul Ricoeur calls 'narrative identity',[5] *The Story of My Life* begins with the need to give an account of what distinguishes the autobiographer from the patchwork of texts that constitute the texture of her mind. There is a change of direction, here – a movement away from *anagnosis:* 'As I look back on my struggle to write that little story, it seems to me that I must have had a prophetic vision of the good that would come of the undertaking, or I should surely have failed' (66). It is a backward glance, a retrospective vision, or moment of hindsight that brings to light the necessity of prophetic vision. This is a version of interpretation that acknowledges an historical imperative, but that uses it to reactivate a past that now appears to be proleptic.

Both 'The Frost King' and this first attempt at autobiography are referred to as 'little stories', the second being a reassertion of the life that was threatened by the textuality of the first, yet also another story, another text. But now, prolepsis is uncovered by *anagnosis*, and it is this apocalypse that effects the return of repressed life. The new emerges at the moment of return: return and escape are not altogether distinct.

6. Freedom

This is a question of freedom. It is never easy to know quite what freedom is in this context, since to be free from the constraints of language, is to be imprisoned in aphasia; to be free from aphasia is to be bound to, and by, language. The Nietzschean version of interpretation, according to Derrida, is the one that pursues a kind of hermeneutic freedom, but it is also the version that severs language from the world and binds us, without mercy in chains of signification (like the one discovered by Weber in the pursuit of dictionary definitions). This paradox is mirrored by that associated with the other kind of interpretation – that which escapes the order of the sign, but which is bound by the limitations of a quest for truth and origin, and is therefore (on Derrida's account) always in exile.

This might be considered in terms of what Ricoeur has called the 'two categories of freedom': freedom from . . . , and freedom for . . . . On the one hand, treating the text as something other than a conglomerate of signs, frees us *from* the semiological structure and its formalistic restrictions, while, on the other hand, it frees us *for* communication. The opposing version of interpretation could be construed as a freedom *from* the pursuit of origins and as a freedom *for* textual play. But, at this point, what appeared at first to be a paradox becomes a flat contradiction, since the notion of inter-pretative play depends (albeit negatively) upon the structural model of language. The very idea of 'play', in its Derridean context, has to do with a certain loosening of what Derrida refers to as 'the structurality of struc-ture,'[6] while the pursuit of non-origins (the Nietzschean genealogies, the Foucauldian archaeologies, and the Derridean etymologies) *denies* the structural model, contravening the synchronic restriction by means of a diachronic research.

You see the difficulty. We are free to read, write, listen, speak and interpret, only insofar as we are also bound by the constraints of whatever inheres in our language: culture, value, conceptuality: escape is return. This means acknowledging that freedom is always in doubt, while recognising that exile from language is truly a less forgiving and inherently more damaging kind of incarceration. Helen Keller's *anagnostic* experience bears witness to the validity of suspicion, even where language seems most like a necessary freedom. It reminds us that language can never be enjoyed as the estate of the individual; it is always already in other mouths, in other systems, on other pages and screens. But if suspicion calls into question, or limits our freedom, that suspicion itself is also a text in need of interpretation; so I can never get to the root of the problem. All I can do is to face up to the *anagnostic* moment, and toggle between graphosclerosis, and prolepsis. Neither freedom nor incarceration, but the running away that is also return.

Hermeneutic freedom (like any other kind) is confronted with, or even differentiated by, certain moments of doubt that may constitute a kind of confinement. The interpreter necessarily occupies a space akin to the chequerboard identified by Browning's Bishop Blougram: 'All we have gained then by our unbelief / Is a life of doubt diversified by faith, / For one of faith diversified by doubt: / We called the chess-board white, – we call it black.'[7] I dare say such agnosticism seems cowardly to some; to others it will appear cynical; for me it is merely necessary. Theory and not theory. Neither and both. The sign is prodigal. You know the story.

7. Another Key

Sometimes writing demands escape. Sometimes escape is miraculous. This is the last key I can find in Cunningham's book. It appears out of the blue when Cunningham describes a moment in Virginia Woolf's *Mrs Dalloway* and then quotes it: 'the sky-writing that pithers away into unreadable alphabetical blur ('But what letters? A C was it? An E, then an L? . . . a K, and E, a Y perhaps?'). Not quite unreadable, is it? Not an alphabetical blur: A-C-E-L-K-E-Y: A CELL KEY. Almost. The second L is missing if we want the word 'cell'. An open cell? Is this the L that Cunningham has previously found (again thanks to an accident of Woolf's text) in 'wor(l)d': the L of a difference that allows Cunningham to speak of the world in the word? We can't be sure that the miraculous key is really there at all; it is conditioned by the doubt about what shape these dubious, airy, evanescent letters take. Interpretation depends upon these moments of seeing: moments at which, in the play of faith and doubt that characterises language, the creative and the critical interact to read a writing, and to write a reading. I have plucked this key out of the air as Helen Keller drew hers from the water.

The Broken Doll

I was wrecked on the way to language, split apart by the unfinished sign. Language arrives as penitence for such dispersion, bearing the scars of an internal scattering.

> Let the unity in the essence of language that we are seeking be called the rift-design. The name calls upon us to descry more clearly what is proper to the essence of language. Riss [rift] is the same word as ritzen [to notch, carve]. We often come across the word Riss in the purely pejorative form, for example as a crack in the wall . . . The rift-design is the drawing of the essence of language, the well-joined structure of a showing in which what is addressed enjoins the speakers and their speech, enjoins the spoken and its unspoken.[1]

Before you lie the dissevered parts of a unjoined structure. Structure *in potentia*. In this dead eye you can see trees, grass, sky, someone passing the window. She will enter the room, gather the pieces, and cry over them, unable to see them or how they might fit together. But something will be born even out of my hopeless case. Someone may stick the bits together. Perhaps someone else will trace the joins, and go on to map the process by which I came to be reassembled. I might become the site of an archaeology.

> If one grants that every signifying practice is a field of transpositions of various signifying systems (an intertextuality), one then understands that its 'place' of enunciation and its denoted 'object' are never single, complete, and identical to themselves, but always plural, shattered . . . [2]

She will come in, smelling of the garden, her hands cold and clean, her fingers crying over me; she will want to put me together again with hands that are wet, slippery, numb.

> A postmodern ethics, in fact, will insist on producing or discovering rifts, gaps, distances, differences, not in order to break up all sense of community but — unendingly — in the interests of a community to come whose values are still to be formulated, a solidarity that has yet to be created.[3]

Can you imagine the reconstructed form? Or are you blind to the relationship between the scattered objects? As I lie shattered, she holds her hand
under running water and the light of the world dawns.

> The path of *analysis*, the decomposition into smaller units, is the very path
> of science, as one sees in the use of the analytic process . . . the reduction to
> simple elements sanctions the elimination of a fundamental function of
> symbolism which can appear only at the higher level of *manifestation* and
> which places symbolism in relation with reality, with experience, with the
> world, with existence . . . [4]

I break like the object of a science; in my disaggregation a meaning gathers;
something other than myself. In the distance, beyond the window, water
runs, like language, over her skin, connecting her with everything. I fall
apart and the light comes in. I must be a symbol – a symbol of all that there
is.

A song is playing in an ear that lies beneath the piano: 'There is a crack,
a crack in everything; that's how the light gets in.'[5]

The left ear, lodged between the bookcase and the radio, hears voices
from another room: 'Here on earth we live on fragments. Our thoughts are
fragments. Our knowledge itself is patchwork.'[6] 'The text is always made
up of a mosaic of conscious and unconscious citation of earlier discourse.'[7]

> **Mosaic** – of or associated with Moses (*OED*).
> **mosaic** – a picture or pattern produced by an arrangement of small
> variously coloured pieces of glass or stone (*OED*).

The left arm split at the elbow, the right resting on the edge of the hearth,
raised to salute the ashes in the grate; a sexless trunk dead centre of the floor;
legs forced apart either side of a crazed eye; indeterminate bits strewn across
a richly figured carpet.

> Being alienated from myself, as painful as that may be, provides me with
> that exquisite distance within which perverse pleasure begins as well as the
> possibility of my imagining and thinking, the impetus of my culture. Split
> identity, kaleidoscope of identities: can we be a saga for ourselves without
> being considered mad or fake?[8]

I am the bits and pieces that fall about in the eyepiece of the kaleidoscope:
chaotic, senseless, random then aligned like a prismatic snowflake. Gone

again. I have escaped the bolts and bars that pinned limb to limb and ordered me to mimic human shape; the strange glue of identity has dissolved.

> The question of the self: 'who am I?' not in the sense of 'who am I?' but the 'who is this "I"' that can say 'who?' What is the 'I', and what becomes of responsibility once the identity of the 'I' trembles *in secret?*[9]

She is the living secret, without language, but on the way to language. As she fingers the pieces, the fragments of my shattered form, she trembles on the verge of knowing, on the verge of turning for home, penitent, sorry for her exile.

What can be made of me? Of these pieces that were once my self? All the parts, reassembled – what would they make? Can I be put together again like the law that Moses broke? Match part with part, align the jagged edges, jut with rut, apex with nadir, and what do you get? Un-lifelike image of a seamy, fractured human? Or the truest android, newly articulate, jointed in unimagined ways, visible at last: 'brittle crazie glass . . . transcendent place'?[10]

The Strange Face of Dr Jekyll and Mr Hyde

'. . . he saw Paul coming, a man small in size, bald-headed,
bandy legged, well-built, with eyebrows meeting, rather
long-nosed, full of grace. For sometimes he looked like a
man, and sometimes he had the countenance of an angel.' [1]

'. . . we cannot even regard ourselves as a constant; in this flux
of things, our identity itself seems in a perpetual variation;
and not infrequently we find our own disguise
the strangest in the masquerade.' [2]

I. The Strangest Disguise

The Strange Case of Doctor Jekyll and Mr Hyde is famously a parable of the
divided or multiplied self; self-division and the interior monologue (or
dialogue) by which it is represented, return us to parables, including that
of the prodigal son. Of course, the parables of Jesus were not the first stories
to use such a device; Greek drama and epic poetry employed interior monologue well before the time of Jesus. But, as Philip Sellew has argued, its use
'in writings of a more historical, philosophical, or rhetorical flavour is rare.'
[3] It is Luke's Jesus in particular who favours this device as a means of drama-
tising the key conflict upon which the force of the parable depends. In the
story of the prodigal son, there is a moment of interior monologue that is
also the moment of turning, conversion, repentance, or realisation:

> When he came to himself, he said, How many hired servants of my father's
> have bread enough and to spare, and I perish with hunger? I will arise and
> go to my father, and will say unto him, Father, I have sinned against heaven,
> and before thee, And am no more worthy to be called thy son: make me as
> one of thy hired servants. (Luke 15: 17–19)

As in Edmund Gosse's *Father and Son*, the internalised father fathers the self,
calling the self out of itself and into dialogue. In the context of its rhetorical situation, the self in Jesus' parable divides not only into the participants

in a three-way conversation between internalised father, speaker and auditor, but into a multiplicity that is not easy to quantify: it occurs within a parable that arises in an argument; it is a *dramatic* moment in a *narrative* intervention in a *discursive* context. The self evoked, then, is a multiple self, dispersed among the layers of discourse in which it is formed. This is not the limit of its complexity; it occurs within a parable that is recounted as part of a larger narrative, which itself has a suasive purpose. It is not difficult to imagine a diagram of boxes within boxes, but I will resist the temptation to produce it, since that would reduce the pleasurable anomie of a lawless subjectivity effected by the coalescence of the critical and the creative. It is after all, in the character of the parable to problematise that important division.

The strangeness of the self recoverable from the parable of the prodigal son is not unfamiliar, though it is rarely traced to the parable. The story goes something like this: modern thinkers, from Descartes on, have often had what can seem like a comparatively clear-eyed view of themselves. Viewing the human mind as the 'mirror of nature', as Richard Rorty puts it, they have included in its reflective field, their own pristine images.[4] Descartes thought his self-reflection clear enough to found an entire philosophical system on: self was the one thing which could not be doubted, and it became the founding idea of modern philosophy.[5] Kant, too, found in his perusal of his own mind sufficient clarity to limn out the entire architecture of reason, drawing on no other source. He wrote in the Preface to the first edition of the *Critique of Pure Reason*: 'I have to deal with nothing save reason and its pure thinking; and to obtain complete knowledge of these, there is no need to go far afield, since I come upon them in my own self.'[6] Subsequently, of course, Nietzsche took a Darwinian hammer to the looking glass, arguing that the Cartesian 'I' was 'only a supposition, an assertion.'[7] Marx went on to breathe the powers of nature and culture onto the mirror of self-representation, pointing to the real-world conditions under which human consciousness is produced: 'Consciousness can never be anything else than conscious existence, and the existence of men is their actual life-process.'[8] The story continues with Freud's insistence that self-representation is superficial, Lacan's claim that it is an effect of language, and Irigaray's perception of it as distorted by gendered conceptions.[9]

Given the barrage of damaging blows aimed at the mirror of self-consciousness, we might say that such suspicious texts have supplanted mirrors: they have shown us an image of ourselves that is unlike both the visual awareness of our appearance, and the figure that appears before our imagination when we reflect upon ourselves. But the chastening of Descartes' and Kant's self images, and the breaking of their vainglorious mirrors, did not require much beside the careful reading of St Paul, whose story is a parable of the multiplying self. Robert Louis Stevenson was, perhaps, among the first to recognise this. Or, at least, the first to encode that recognition in fictional form. In that most Pauline of tales, *The Strange Case of Dr Jekyll and Mr Hyde*, subjectivity is explored in a way that both echoes Paul's text, and brings to light the puzzling fecundity of the self. A series of reflections pass between the texts of Stevenson and Paul, creating an image of the Christian subject, or any other prodigal self.

In the process of discovering this image, another reflection is produced: the inversion of William James' account of conversion in *The Varieties of Religious Experience*. He describes the process as one of the reunification of a divided subject:

> To be converted, to be regenerated, to receive grace, to experience religion, to gain an assurance, are so many phrases which denote the process, gradual or sudden, by which a self hitherto divided, and consciously wrong inferior and unhappy, becomes unified and consciously right superior and happy, in consequence of its firmer hold upon religious realities.[10]

The subject of conversion that emerges from the current exploration moves in the opposing direction: towards the splitting, or disaggregation, of the self. It is precisely this fracturing within the self, and the echoes of St Paul that can be detected in its delineation, that make *Jekyll and Hyde* a peculiarly instructive narrative in the consideration of conversion and subjectivity.

Stevenson's interest in the multiplicity of the self pre-dates the publication of *Jekyll and Hyde* by at least five years. In an essay entitled 'Crabbed Age and Youth' (1881), Stevenson pondered the changes that come about with age, observing that they can occasionally be drastic, amounting, at times, to reversals. He himself, the essay tells us, was once a socialist, but he tended towards conservatism as he grew older. In the course of Stevenson's discussion of changes affecting personality, St Paul is used as an example of extreme alteration in the subject: ' . . . if St Paul had not been a very zealous Pharisee, he would have been a colder Christian.'[11] Leaving aside the questions of historical accuracy in Stevenson's assertion, it is possible to note that he saw the crisis of the Damascene moment as being characterised by both change and continuity; despite the extreme nature of the event, something of Paul's character as a Christian (warmth, or passion) was traceable to something in his pre-conversion identity (zeal). Such continuity-in-discontinuity would later find its way into the strange, unsettling description of self-division in *Jekyll and Hyde*. But Stevenson's story owes a lot more to the writings of Paul than an interest in the idea that something survives the most radical change within the self.

A little later in the same essay, Stevenson seems to be more exercised by the greatness of *differences* within the self than by any putative continuity: ' . . . we cannot even regard ourselves as a constant; in this flux of things, our identity itself seems in a perpetual variation; and not infrequently we find our own disguise the strangest in the masquerade.'[12] Here, there is a sense of change that defies the very idea of subjective continuity; a kind of auto-alienation is implied, by which the self is turned into another: a disguised other: the strangest other of all. The complexity of such a description, which characterises subjectivity as a masquerade in which the self is an all-but unrecognisable stranger, a figure of auto-dissimulation, might be read as preparing the way for the manifold subjectivity and self-estrangement with which the reader of *Jekyll and Hyde* would be confronted some five years later. Before exploring the detail of Stevenson's story of multiple identity, I want to turn to the writings of St Paul in order to trace out its provenance.

2. 'No More I'

Throughout his writings, St Paul raises issues of self-awareness, that stem from his own self-division in the process of conversion. Whether in his self-aggrandising autobiographical narratives, or in his finger-pointing homilies, he is ever trying to raise some kind of textual mirror before his readers. He points out, on one occasion, that self-consciousness is not necessarily truth-telling: 'I judge not mine own self. For I know nothing by myself; yet am I not hereby justified: but he that judgeth me is the Lord' (1 Cor. 4:3–4). Nevertheless, he advocates a high degree of self-scrutiny, urging on the Roman believers, for example, the need to look coldly upon themselves: 'For I say . . . to every man that is among you, not to think of himself more highly than he ought to think; but to think soberly, according as God hath dealt to every man the measure of faith' (Rom. 12:3 KJV).

Perhaps the most interesting (certainly the most complex) of Paul's mirror texts, is that astoundingly convoluted description of the battle between rival selves in Romans 7. Despite its difficulty, the passage has been of great significance in the shaping of subjectivity wherever the writ of Christian thought has run. Who is not familiar with images of the good self in dialogue with the bad self? This kind of dualism, frequently mapped onto a hierarchy of body and soul, unites the Platonic and Christian traditions, and reappears at the origins of modern philosophy in the Cartesian ego. But the dualistic interpretation of Paul's text is looking into a darkened glass;

it sees little of the detail. For Romans 7, for all its apparent commitment to a radical distinction between the flesh and the spirit, is far from dualistic in its implications. Paul, we may recall, is at pains to describe in that passage, the desperate struggle between what he calls 'the inward man' (KJV), and the carnal self. But, there is a third self which, according to what might be called the reflexive logic of auto-narrative, observes the fight, and which speaks of both the 'inward man' and 'the flesh', in the third person.

That this is more than a mere accident of Paul's text, can be seen in the way that it is replicated in St Augustine's treatment of Christian subjectivity in the process of conversion. Jill Robbins observes that a certain doubleness is inherent in the very nature of the conversion narrative:

> The *Confessions* already has a built in doubleness: it distinguishes between Augustine the already converted narrator and Augustine the subject of the narrative (the great sinner on his way to conversion). At the moment of conversion the sinner becomes the converted narrator, an 'I' who is able to tell the story of its self-loss and self-recovery. This kind of division of the self, the possibility of losing or finding oneself in a succession of 'moments', is the condition of possibility of personal history and the writing of that history . . . . Every narrative of conversion, which reviews a life from the vantage point of its ending and endows it with retrospective coherence, also demands a dual viewpoint. The partial view of the experiencing subject, blinded by sin, is contrasted with the totalizing viewpoint of the converted narrator . . . [13]

Robbins' point is germane, but does not, perhaps, go quite far enough in distinguishing the multiplicity of Augustine's selfhood. In Book VIII of his *Confessions*, Augustine writes: 'So these two wills, one old, one new, one carnal, the other spiritual, contended with each other and disturbed my soul.'[14] It is difficult to say exactly how many Augustines inhabit these words, but there are *at least three*: the carnal Augustine, the spiritual Augustine, and the observing consciousness who speaks of 'my soul'. The very phrase 'my soul' suggests more than one self since it includes a possessor and a possessed. Furthermore, if the soul itself is a third agency troubled by the conflict between carnal and spiritual selves, then the possessor of the soul is actually a fourth self, possibly identical with the observing consciousness.

Just how many selves are encoded in Paul's text is even less clear. Consider again his familiar characterisation of the inner struggle:

> For I know that in me (that is, in my flesh) dwelleth no good thing: for to

will is present with me; but how to perform that which is good I find not. For the good that I would I do not: but the evil which I would not, that I do. Now if I do that I would not, it is no more I that do it, but sin that dwelleth in me. (Rom. 7: 18–20)

The 'I' here seems to be a narrative effect, imposing a restless unity upon a congeries of unruly agents: me, my flesh, will, sin. The repeated use of 'I', in fact, masks a variety of functions: the narrative, sense-making voice, the desire to do good, the agent which contravenes the desire to do good, are all encrypted in the 'I', which becomes so over-determined that it splits off into a personified 'sin' dwelling in a (by now overcrowded) 'me'.

If, as the Epistle of James suggests, scripture is a mirror (Jas. 1: 23–5), then its glass is broken by Paul's text, as it shows us multiple images of a dynamic, conflictual selfhood. There seems to me to be little doubt that the complicated inner conflict described by Paul in Romans 7, lies beneath Stevenson's depiction of the splitting of Henry Jekyll. This was noted as long ago as 1912, by John Kelman:

> Popular religion adopted the allegory [of Jekyll and Hyde] partly because it was a modern echo of St Paul's words to the Romans, in which the apostle describes himself as leading the double life of unwilling sin and unfulfilled desire for holiness . . . . In this mysterious twofoldness of the inner life it was felt that Stevenson, like St Paul before him, had exposed the root of all our moral difficulties.[15]

Of course, Kelman's 'mysterious twofoldness of the inner life', is something of an understatement. As has already been argued, 'twofoldness' hardly describes the multiplicity of Paul's interior agon. So, if Kelman is right, then he is also wrong. That is to say: if Paul does indeed provide the model for Henry Jekyll's troublesome subjectivity, then we might expect to find not just two sides to Stevenson's protagonist, but a multiplicity of personae associated with the good/bad doctor.

The reflections of Pauline subjective multiplicity that concern me here are not in any straightforward way the products of a personal attachment that binds Stevenson to Paul, although he did grow up in a home where the Bible was read, and religious observance was strictly imposed.[16] Rather, they occur at a variety of levels: historical, structural, cultural, rhetorical, and thematic. The structural splitting of the narrative between a number of distinct voices, mirrors its composition history. For, historically, Stevenson's novella is itself a split entity: there were, appropriately enough, two distinct versions of it: the first, a deliberately sensationalist story, thrown into the fire by Stevenson after his wife's insistence that he could (and should) turn it into a powerful allegory; the second, the published version.[17] The will-to-allegory, moulded by Paul's cardinal distinction between the spirit and the letter, is, of course, a well-documented feature of Christian hermeneutics. In that context, allegory is an interpretative strategy which performs upon the biblical text the kind of splitting here associated with the human psyche. Just as the twin meanings of the text (literal and figural) came to be subdivided into ever more elaborate refinements of sense by patristic and medieval interpreters, it would seem that the Christian psyche had undergone a parallel superfetation by the time Stevenson analysed it. Just how fertile this process could be, I hope to show.

Culturally, the story of Jekyll and Hyde is divided by being simultaneously both familiar and unfamiliar. Edwin Eigner tells the tale of this division between the text and the myth that it spawned:

> *Jekyll and Hyde* has developed into a popular myth, one of the very few to come out of the Victorian period, and its meanings have consequently become blurred. The story was vulgarized within a year of its publication by T.R. Sullivan's popular and sensationalist stage interpretation . . . there were three successful movie versions . . . each one did its bit to coarsen Stevenson's ideas. In quite another way, the story was allegorized almost out of existence by the sermons and leading articles in religious newspapers of the late 1880s. The result is that the term Jekyll-and-Hyde, even as used by psychologists, has little reference to Stevenson's work.[18]

This division is, once again, at least in part, the product of a certain kind of Christian allegory-making, which helped to fashion this 'vulgarized' or 'coarsened' version of the tale. That this 'vulgar' version remains part of the repertoire of British cultural life, could be seen a few years ago in the way that the press in the United Kingdom reported the case of Harold Shipman – a doctor from a place called Hyde (in the city of Manchester) who murdered a yet-to-be-determined number of his patients over many years of practice. Just about every national newspaper referred to the mass murderer (somewhat crassly) as 'The Doctor Jekyll of Hyde'. What the public were meant to understand by the allusion, I presume, was that the doctor in question was a depraved character whose outward professional respectability cloaked his murderous proclivities. The subtext seems to have been that the split personality is a dangerous aberration for which our culture has a suitably cautionary myth – or appropriate parable. In fact, in its role as cultural myth, the story of Doctor Jekyll and Mr Hyde provides us with one of the very few popular images of subjectivity in crisis. Even so, despite the kind of popular perceptions played upon by the British press, Stevenson, drawing on St Paul, depicted the divided self as a commonplace, rather than as an aberration. Even the characterisation of Utterson, the irreproachable and abstemious lawyer, depicts a man divided between an austere self control and a love of wine and the theatre. Of course, this is a familiar theme in Victorian literature. What makes Stevenson's story a particularly interesting case is that it relates this commonplace motif to a specific Christian source, and thus offers a way of approaching some of the key issues in subjectivity as it has been produced in western cultures.

Unlike the journalistic reductions implicit in media representations of the Shipman case, Stevenson indicates the irreducible complexity of subjectivity, weaving for us a multi-voiced narrative, at the heart of which is the profound mystery of human personality. It is structured to delay until as late as possible in the story, the revelation of the actual identity of the doctor and his alter ego. The effect is achieved by the use of multiple viewpoints, the last of which is the confessional account of Dr Jekyll himself. Had the whole narrative been in Jekyll's voice, there would have been no mystery, no narrative tension building to the revelatory moment in which Jekyll discloses his own culpability. Again, the unspecified narrative voice which tells the first part of story could, conceivably, have been allowed to narrate throughout the novella, but not without sacrificing the strange and potent sense of unease which arises when the story of a split self is finally told in the first person. What interests me here, of course, is the provisionality of the term 'first person' in this context.

3. Jekyll's Mirror

A key problem of Stevenson's story, on this reading, is that of Christian subjectivity: what is a self as understood in Christian terms? The problem, as I have already intimated, goes deep and can be traced back to the writings of St Paul, and, possibly even further – to the parable of the prodigal son. The twice-named apostle depicts a self divided between good and evil impulses in perpetual conflict, and proposes a highly problematical split between mind and flesh in response. Stevenson's modern account is chemically based, as Dr Jekyll turns to a kind of substance misuse in order to overcome the Pauline division in nature by which he is plagued. He clearly alludes to Romans 7 in setting up the conflict, referring to 'the perennial war among my members'. But, while Paul's concern is to release the good self from its thrall to the bad, Jekyll seeks to emancipate the bad self from the good – to be two distinct people rather than one unified self controlled by good impulses. Furthermore, despite a Platonic-Pauline tone in the description of the drug's effect, Jekyll's character does not split neatly along the putative body-spirit faultline associated with a certain Christian-metaphysical tradition. This is Jekyll's account of the effects of his designer chemical agent:

> . . . I not only recognised my natural body for the mere aura and effulgence of certain powers that made up my spirit, but managed to compound a drug by which these powers should be dethroned from their supremacy, and a second form and countenance substituted, none the less natural to me because they were the expression, and bore the stamp, of lower elements in my soul.[19]

A Pauline topography of the self is subjected to a pseudo-scientific intervention, here, to produce a kind of non-explanation. The *body* is made to mirror the *soul* by means of a drug which seems to act chiefly upon the *spirit*. The very idea that a physical substance could impact upon the spirit, 'dethrones' the spirit by inverting the hierarchy of the dualistic system in which nothing physical can act upon the spiritual, since the higher cannot be acted upon by the lower. Thus Stevenson's text destabilises the very economy upon which its formulation of subjectivity is based. I would argue that this destabilisation is not an innovation in Stevenson; rather, it reiterates Paul's formulation by covering the field of the unreflected in the Pauline corpus. For, the same instability is evident in Paul's rhetoric, especially at the point where he needs to distinguish clearly between the flesh and the spirit, as in 1 Corinthians 3:14. There Paul addresses the Corinthians as fleshly or 'carnal' rather than 'spiritual' precisely because they cannot be fed on flesh. Meat, the extrapolation of flesh, is (paradoxically) reserved for the 'spiritual'. This chiasmus makes *flesh* appropriate only to the *spiritual*, who would seem to have little use for it, and denies it to the *fleshly,* whose condition would suggest dependence upon it. In splitting flesh from its own cognate (meat), and aligning it with the spirit, Paul's rhetoric disrupts the fundamental distinction between flesh and spirit upon which Christian dualism depends. Thus when Jekyll creates a physical substance that acts upon the spirit, he is reinscribing Paul's insistence upon feeding meat to the spiritual. And if the hierarchy between flesh and spirit is thus compromised in such a crucial gesture, it is not to be wondered at that the subjectivity constructed upon it fractures and falls apart. This is what can be seen to take place in Romans 7, and it happens again in *Jekyll and Hyde.*

The chemical compound, Jekyll tells the reader, 'shook the very fortress of identity' and threatened spiritual death. This trembling fortress is echoed a few pages later by a shaking jail – not just any old wobbly jail, but that specific Philippian jail that once failed to hold Paul in his cell: 'The drug had no discriminating action; it was neither diabolical nor divine; it but shook the doors of the prisonhouse of my disposition; and like the captives of Philippi, that which stood within ran forth' (Stevenson, *JH*: 85). This odd misreading of the incident recorded in Acts 16 (according to which there was no 'running forth'), potentially alerts the reader to a certain kind of textual reflection.

There are repeated suggestions that Jekyll views his alter ego as enjoying an unprecedented *freedom* in his separation from the unified being. Not only is the drug characterised as a means of *escape* from the prisonhouse of the compound disposition, but its effects are the reduction of inhibition, and a 'disordering of sensual images', producing what Jekyll characterises as *freedom* without innocence. Hyde is described as '*delivered* from the aspirations and remorse of his more upright twin' (85), as springing headlong into the sea of *liberty* (86), and as 'struggling after *freedom*' (90) (emphasis added). It adds up to the representation of Jekyll as Hyde's erstwhile jailer. Just as in the story of the prodigal, it is the act of escaping that splits the self apart; or is it the splitting of the self that actually constitutes escape? Either way, it is unsurprising that Hyde's escape should evoke Paul and Silas' quaking prison. But what of the misrepresentation in the suggestion that the captives of Philippi 'ran forth' like Hyde? It is an important distortion, for the prisoners' refusal to take advantage of their good fortune is a key aspect of the conversion narrative in Acts. Had the prisoners taken to their heels, the jailer would have killed himself and would not have been converted; his suicide is prevented only by Paul's shout: 'Don't harm yourself! We are all here!' (Acts 16:28, NIV). Hyde's escape has precisely the effect of leading his jailer (Jekyll) to a kind of suicide, complete with suicide note – his written confession. The incident recorded in Acts 16 leads to the conversion to Christian faith of the jailer and his family, precisely because the inmates did not 'run forth', so the fact that Stevenson's text misses the point, draws attention to Hyde's escape as a negative conversion narrative – a narrative of deconversion, as the 'pure evil' of Hyde gradually becomes dominant. The rhetorical structure of the prison affair, it seems, raises what might be represented as a distorted mirror image in which Mr Hyde is the grotesquely misshapen reflection of Paul.

The following physical description of the apostle, taken from the second-century work, *The Acts of Paul and Thecla,* can be seen to add another dimension to the image of Paul in Stevenson's text: ' . . . he saw Paul coming, a man small in size, bald-headed, bandy legged, well-built, with eyebrows meeting, rather long-nosed, full of grace. For sometimes he looked like a man, and sometimes he had the countenance of an angel.'[20] R.L. Cross claims that this verbal portrait was decisive for representations of Paul in Christian art.[21] Whether or not Stevenson knew of such a description, its cultural presence can be said to augment the perception that Paul's image is present in the reflective field of *Jekyll and Hyde*. The observation of the human and the inhuman combining in Paul's countenance, and the evocation of his size and sheer ugliness, find curious parallels in Stevenson's descriptions of Mr Hyde: 'Mr Hyde was pale and dwarfish . . . '; ' . . . the man seems hardly human . . . if ever I saw Satan's signature upon a face, it is on that of your new friend!' (40). The reflective distortions might be tabulated thus:

Paul	Hyde
angelic	demonic
does not escape	escapes
Jailer	Jekyll
converted	deconverted

But, of course, Paul *does* escape in a different sense, for he too divided between Saul and Paul, moving in what might be construed as the opposite direction to that followed by Jekyll/Hyde. The parallel is a complex one: when Hyde (the product of deconversion) escapes, he is compared to an already converted Paul who refuses escape; but the allusion reminds the reader of Paul's self-division and his escape from the person of Saul. So, the disjuncture offers the reader a curiously distorted reflection: it becomes a parable of unmasterable, or uncontainable self-diffraction. The model of exchange between the texts is prodigal, not only in that it tells the story of a self that associates escape with self-division, but also in that Stevenson's tale both escapes and returns to its biblical sources.

The reflection of Paul is played out in the multiplying of Jekyll's personae, as it mirrors the psychological fecundity of Romans 7. The very title given to Jekyll's narrative ('Henry Jekyll's Full Account of the Case'), is steadily ironised (in its claim to fullness) by the reproducing subject in that narrative. An intensifying instability of voice and personae testify to the difficulty. Jekyll is said to remain 'that incongruous compound' of Jekyll and Hyde, while Hyde is 'pure evil' (which potential oxymoron might itself give us pause). The confusion of identity becomes particularly obvious when there is a mirror involved:

> . . . when I looked upon that ugly idol in the glass, I was conscious of no
> repugnance, rather of a leap of welcome. This, too, was myself. It seemed
> natural and human. In my eyes it bore a livelier image of the spirit, it seemed
> more express and single, than the imperfect and divided countenance I had
> been hitherto accustomed to call mine. And in so far I was doubtless right.
> I have observed that when I wore the countenance of Edward Hyde, none
> could come near to me without a visible misgiving of the flesh. (84–5)

We know already that the narrative 'I' is not an undifferentiated Jekyll, for
it has just named both Jekyll and Hyde in the third person. But here, curiously, *Jekyll* seems to be standing before the mirror and seeing *Hyde* in the
glass, so the narrative 'I' occupies an impossible position. Indeed,
throughout the whole of Henry Jekyll's narrative, the 'I' shifts silently
between participant roles: sometimes it appears to be the mysterious third
person who views both Jekyll and Hyde objectively (even expressing a pref-
erence for Jekyll over Hyde at one point: 90); at other times the compound
figure in whom both Jekyll and Hyde reside seems to be narrating; on yet
other occasions, a residual, de-Hyded Jekyll takes up the story. On one occasion, Hyde himself seems to speak in the first person, yet in the passage just
quoted, the image of Hyde is objectified as an 'it' which is also 'myself'.
Again, although the image is *more* the narrator's self than the 'divided countenance' in which Jekyll has a share, the 'I' only 'wears the countenance' of
Hyde. Hyde, then, is both more interior and more exterior than the 'I' for
which he is both subject and object. In other words, not only has Jekyll
divided between the observing third 'I', the compound figure, and a character to be distinguished from Hyde, but Hyde too has divided between
subject and object, between spirit and countenance. No wonder the
narrator, whoever he is, says at one point: 'I cannot say "I"'(94).

Thus, without knowing it, Jekyll fulfils his own prophecy. He has
predicted that human subjectivity will eventually be known to be protean:

> . . . man is not truly one, but truly two. I say two, because the state of my
> own knowledge does not pass beyond that point. Others will follow, others
> will outstrip me on the same lines; and I hazard the guess that man will be
> ultimately known for a mere polity of multifarious, incongruous and inde-
> pendent denizens. (82)

Jekyll himselves is no more confined to a mere twosome than was the patron
saint of the divided self: Saul/Paul.

4. Paul's Mirror

A curious aspect of Stevenson's reflection of Paul is that the de-conversion of Jekyll has much the same consequences for subjectivity as the conversion of Saul/Paul: both shake into fragments an already flawed psyche. Were we to follow William James's model of conversion as re-integration, we might expect de-conversion to be precisely what the story of Henry Jekyll suggests: disintegration. But Stevenson's use of Paul draws the Pauline model of conversion into the process of deconversion, so that, in the economy of *Jekyll and Hyde* deconversion is not the reversal of conversion, but a species of it. For Jekyll's disintegration begins with a Pauline perception of internal disharmony, and proceeds towards the kind of psychic multiplicity Paul describes in Romans 7. Of course, some would argue that the Pauline passage in question deals with a 'pre-conversion' condition, but even if that were the case (and this is far from certain), Paul's narrations of his name-changing encounter with Christ, imply that conversion does not heal the inner rifts; rather, it renders them permanent, if not eternal. For example, in Galatians, after recounting the story of his conversion, he insists: ' . . . I live; yet not I, but Christ liveth in me . . . ' Like Stevenson's compound narrative voice, the converted Paul could not say 'I', at least, not without needing to negate it, to supplant it with 'not I'. And yet it is precisely the badge of selfhood, the autobiographical narrative, the individuation of Paul as an authentic minister and apostle, that gives rise to its opposite: self-negation. The problem is one of the deep logic of conversion: if the 'I' is sacrificed, then who, or what, is saved? Paul's formulation might even be said to raise a mirror image of the cross, in which Christ's death for the life of the individual, is met with the death of the individual for the continuing life of Christ. The death of the individual is also the birth of the shifting, centreless, protean self.

Paul's famous mirror, then, the darkened glass of 1 Corinthians 13:12, in which we see a dim image of Christ, is much more than a metaphor for imperfect knowledge of the divine; it also reflects an unclear, clouded subjectivity of the kind that emerges in Stevenson's Victorian myth. For, the self has become indistinguishable from Christ-in-me, but Paul's text actually admits that the blurred image of Christ is also a failure of self-knowledge. The verse in question runs: 'For now we see through a glass, darkly; but then face to face: now I know in part; but then I shall know even as also I am known.' Just as Jekyll looks into the mirror and sees a recognisable, but altered, image which confounds all boundaries of selfhood, Paul sees behind his darkened glass a moment of self-revelation which is also a face-to-face encounter with the other: 'I live; yet not I,' indeed. The revelation of selfhood that Paul projects beyond the image in the glass – the knowing as *I am known* – is nothing but what the darkened glass itself shows him. This is the logic of his insistence that *'now* we see through a glass darkly': there is, after all, no time but the present, no moment but now, from which to reflect upon the future. Every insistence about the future falls within that conditioning, circumscribed, and shadowy 'now'.

A distorted reflection of this distorted reflection appears in *Jekyll and Hyde* as the double mirror image that is both startlingly clear and revelatory, that offers the sharpest possible view of selfhood – 'a livelier image of the spirit', and yet is no more than a mist, an obfuscating breath which darkens the glass: 'Edward Hyde,' says the narrator of Jekyll's polyphonic confession, 'would pass away like the stain of breath upon a mirror' (86).

Reason's Disciple
After Master Derrida

---

disciple   a follower or pupil of a leader, teacher, philosophy etc.
2 any early believer in Christ, esp. one of the twelve Apostles.
(*OED*)

Kiss the Son lest he be angry, and ye perish from the way.
(Ps. 2:12, *KJV*)

. . . he came to Jesus and said, 'Hail, Master;' and he kissed Him.
(Matt. 26:49, *KJV*)

Difference is articulation.
(Jacques Derrida, *Of Grammatology*)

I. Some versions of Judas

Jorge Luis Borges's *Labyrinths* includes a parable entitled 'Three Versions of Judas', which explores Christianity's interpretative problem with the treacherous disciple.[1] Judas is lodged in Christian tradition as both the damned betrayer of Jesus and as a figure necessary to the scheme of salvation. He is a hand-picked companion of the Son of the God, and yet his nefarious dealings with the powers that be, lead to Jesus' arrest and execution – an execution upon which hinges our salvation. Judas either plays into the hands of a scheming God, or acts as a conscious and willing agent in the soteriological drama. Borges picks up on the fact that the Christian tradition has always been, to some extent, unsure what to make of him. The more orthodox interpretations cited by Borges include the following: Judas betrayed Jesus out of greed – he did it for the money; he was predestined to damnation – a mere pawn in the game of Redemption; he was a zealot who thought to spur Jesus into open political rebellion against Rome. Of course, some of these alternatives might lead one to question Jesus' judgement in taking up with Judas in the first place. But the focus of Borges's parable is the much more interesting, heretical idea that Judas was a kind of martyr: he chose to sacrifice his own spirit in an act of absolute asceticism: to damn himself to hell in order to make salvation possible.

One thing that emerges from this consideration of Judas, is that the very idea of discipleship, of following a master, is never straightforward or unproblematical. Judas is both disciple and anti-disciple, both follower and not follower, irreducibly: he does not cease to be a disciple simply because he betrays the master. His betrayal may have been an act of the highest devotion. Similarly, acts of the highest devotion may be betrayals. Is this not what Friedrich Nietzsche pointed out in his characterisation of 'the most dangerous party member', in *Human, All Too Human*, the one who by an 'all too devout pronouncement of the party principles, provokes others to apostasy'? [2]

In a sense, Judas is actually the archetypal disciple. I am thinking of a remark made by Paul Ricoeur, in his reading of Mark's gospel: 'It is not correct to say that Judas alone is the only opponent . . . Everyone betrays, denies, flees . . .'[3] Disciples are unruly creatures. They may fall asleep on you in the hour of your greatest need, or they may swear allegiance unto death, only to deny all knowledge of you the next morning. They may turn your memory into a religion, or rewrite your rebellion and hetero-doxy as an ideology of obedience. They may even sell you to your enemies. What, then, does it mean to follow in the sense in which one might be said to follow a leader, teacher, or philosophy? We probably have two models – one from religion, the other from philosophy. Both seem to me to be troubled by what we might call the Judas principle, or, to give it its rhetorical name: *anacoluthon*.

2. Anacoluthon

Anacoluthon, from *akoluthia*, meaning follower, or disciple. From this root we get our word 'acolyte'. The negative prefix an- , then suggests a following (or follower) which (or who) does not follow. But perhaps all following is captured by anacoluthon, since all joining involves the point of articulation, the partial bridging of interstices which marks both the uniting and the dividing of object with object, or subject with subject. Perhaps the acolyte both follows and does not follow in the same movement. Instability is inherent in the connection in which one person or thing attaches to, joins, or cleaves to another. The double meaning of 'cleaving' – sundering and adhering – reveals the ambiguity of relation.

The disciple or acolyte is a cultural predicate, attached and detached by an unstable bond, seam, hinge to/from the master, founder or forerunner: connected by an articulation which is, by definition, un*master*able. We might say that the disciple is the follower/not follower, the devout betrayer, constituted by a belatedness, a coming after. The disciple may seek to repeat, double, reiterate, amplify, elucidate, continue or complete the founder's project, only to find themselves subject to the heretical necessity of articulation. To articulate is, as Master Derrida has observed, both to join and to sever.[4] The more articulate the disciple, we might say, the greater the risk or promise of heresy. Wherever the disciple *articulates* their *following*, a double-jointedness occurs, whereby the text subjects to juncture/disjuncture for a second time, the following/not following of a personal attachment/detachment. The unruly disciple swings both ways.

3. Reason's disciple

Reason's disciple is, typically, the follower who does not follow, who betrays merely by following. So, Plato betrays Socrates by writing, poisoning his system in trespassing against its proscription, and, by the very same means, curing him – rescuing him from oblivion with the memorial of written dialogues. I am following Derrida, here, of course.[5] Plato himself is then betrayed by Aristotle, who resolutely refuses to deny reality to the material world, who studies Nature and who writes the *Physics*. And so it goes.

Curiously, such diversions from the way of the founder, which constitute progress in the articulation of reason, are forgotten or occluded in its methods. So, the syllogism, in its touching commitment to the chain of predications, represses the memory of betrayal or deviation, and thus it always, in a certain way, brings to light a failure to follow. Since a predicate may always not follow, may be unruly, tangential, or elliptical, articulation in the form of predication always subjects the syllogism to the presence of its other – anacoluthon. Anacoluthon is, perhaps, the anti-syllogism, the return of the repressed in the articulation of reason. It brings to light the slippage between thought and expression, naming the gap or dehiscence of which expression is itself the predicate.

4. Heretical orthodoxy

Reason always implies anacoluthon. Reasoned argument, that is to say, is the determination of what follows. Does the conclusion follow from the premis(es)? 'Does it necessarily follow?' we ask when we want to question an argument, or disrupt a discourse. 'Do you follow?' the master asks the pupil. These questions are always unanswerable, for following is unmasterable – it is that which the master cannot predict, foreclose, or determine. By what instantaneously repetitive exchange might it be known? To trace a trajectory from implication to inference and back, to replicate and continue a movement of thought, would be to undo the situatedness of both the founder and the follower, to perform a groundless manoeuvre in air. Since the thought of the founder and that of the follower are necessarily discontinuous, the mastery of a following would demand an act of divination, in defiance of reason. Is the history of ideas, in this sense, the history of divination? An heretical orthodoxy? Anacoluthon?

5. The Founder

The founder swings from the same unstable hinge as the disciple, in the dangerous promise of what follows/does not follow. The founder is only a founder inasmuch as a following can be established. Founding is thus always also finding. The founder must find in the disciple, already taking place, that which forms in the founding. There is no founding without discipleship, no Socrates without Plato, no Christ without Judas. The founder then is constituted by the belatedness of discipleship, always already betrayed by the act of founding/finding. Like the disciple, the founder is thus captured by anacoluthon: having to share both the belatedness of the finding and the inaugurating or bringing to light of the found(ed).

6. I must follow

Modern philosophy is distinguished as that which does not follow; it breaks with what precedes it. Thus we find Descartes, the solitary founder, beginning his *Discourse on Method* with the determination not to be a follower:

> . . . there came a day when I resolved to make my studies within myself, and use all my powers of mind to choose the paths I must follow. This undertaking, I think, succeeded much better than it would have if I had never left my country or my books.[6]

Already Descartes is both following and not following: looking for a path, a way already marked out and trodden, but turning away from predecessors, leaving behind his country and, most significantly, his books. He looks inside himself for the already trodden way which 'I must follow'. 'I' is famously what does follow. And it follows precisely because Descartes does not follow. It is his refusal to follow that leads to the *'cogito ergo sum'*. The 'I' is, characteristically a follower, produced by not following. It is uncovered in a solitude that is stressed by Descartes' text in order to mask the discipleship of the ego. Descartes tells us that he shut himself up inside a stove in order to find within himself the object of his study.

In the warmth and silence, a thought articulates itself: the thought of articulation, or, more precisely of an articulation which hides its own articulacy under a series of putative unities:

> One of the first things I thought it well to consider was that as a rule there is not such great perfection in works composed of several parts, and proceeding from the hands of various artists, as in those on which one man has worked alone.[7]

As though to legitimate the choice of solitary speculation, the disavowal of multiplicity in production and constitution represses articulation, joining, combination. It attempts to seize the hinge, to establish fixity and continuity – an untroubled passage for discourse which would render the 'I am' a necessary corollary of the 'I think', the *ergo* becoming translucent, almost invisible. But its visibility is re-established by the admission that this was not the first thing, but 'one of the first things' presenting itself to the 'I': one thing selecting itself, as if by chance, out of a multiplicity; one thing, detached, unitary, apparently *sui generis*. Yet, the principle of selection is the solitariness of the 'I', the masking of its following, the legitimation of its not following.

Solitariness selects solitariness as its starting point. Where else can the founder find what is needed? Here, in the warmth of the stove, the enclosed self disavows all exterior influence, gestating itself in a not following of the world beyond. Yet the stove, external, environmental, the space around, becomes the figure of internal self-enclosure necessary to the birth of the ego. The inner space derives from the outer in a kind of ergonomics of the self.

*Ergo*nomics. This co-implication of inner and outer space must be replicated within the *ergo* – the predicating of the 'I am' upon the 'I think', for the solitariness constituted by the external space gives rise to the 'I think'. The movement from outer to inner crosses through the *ergo*. We might ask, then, if the *ego* follows the *cogito*. What would such a following mean? Is the *ergo*, lodged between the thinking self and the found, or thought self, masterable by the *ego*? We know that the *cogito* is already a following/not following since it has been constituted by the leaving of books and country, and by the finding of a path. Is the ego another double-jointed disciple?

We may be reminded once again of Nietzsche. In *Beyond Good and Evil* there is this meditation upon the predication of the ego:

A thought comes when 'it' will and not when 'I' will. It is thus a falsification of the evidence to say that the subject 'I' conditions the predicate 'think'. It is thought, to be sure, but that this 'it' should be that old famous 'I' is, to put it mildly, only a supposition, an assertion.[8]

In Descartes' meditation, that 'it' sends itself towards the *ego* in the articulatory moment of the *ergo*. It enables the predication of the *ego*, allowing it to emerge from the *cogito*, to follow and to not follow the *cogito*. Anacoluthon brings to light a certain logic in Nietzsche's claim, turning what he calls a supposition into precisely the matter of 'grammatical custom' that he insists it is.

7. Kantian ergonomics

Who follows Descartes? Who does not? Kant repeats Descartes' decision to follow none but himself. In this, he necessarily both follows and does not follow Descartes. The Preface to the first edition of the *Critique of Pure Reason* contains the following Cartesian gesture: 'I have to do with nothing save reason and its pure thinking; and to obtain complete knowledge of these, there is no need to go far afield, since I come upon them in my own self.' [9] In place of Descartes' abandoned books, Kant informs the reader that he has rejected those 'writers [who] pledge themselves to extend human knowledge beyond all limits of possible experience.' [10] In place of Descartes' distant country, is Kant's not needing 'to go far afield'. Descartes' sense of distance from influence is not, it seems, necessary to Kant, since he is not tasked with finding the self which is to be the subject of exploration. This is, presumably, because Descartes had already found it (in Germany, of course). As Descartes found within himself the ego's path, Kant finds 'reason and its pure thinking' gestating within his 'own self'. Reason, then, seems to occupy the anacoluthic space of the following, not following ego, discipled to the found and founding self.

Kant's reasoning is, then, *ergo*nomic, both in the sense of its adaptation to its environment – its comfortable location within himself, and in the sense that it follows the law of the Cartesian *ergo*. One might rewrite his *mise en scene* thus: 'I find reason and its pure thinking in my own self, therefore (ergo) I do not need to go far afield'. Once more, the question of predication troubles the solitude of the thinker, who, resisting, but also establishing, a distance between reason and the ego, tries to connect without mediation, only to find the breach already there. The exteriority which crosses though Descartes' *ergo* appears again in Kant's, this time in negative form as an unspecified, and therefore unquantifiable, proximity. Distance is reduced, but not overcome. So, the Cartesian *ergo* becomes the one and only conduit of reason, and once again it belongs both to the inside and the outside of the self. It remains within the grasp of an irreducible anacoluthon: it can never be resolved into either a following or a not following. Is reason always in a sense an ergonomics? How comfortably does it pass through the *ergo*?

8. Writing and ergonomics

Is it, perhaps the technicity of writing that enables Descartes and Kant to enclose reason within their own ergonomically designed egological structures? It is, after all, the contiguity of space and time in the unity of an experience that brings to light both the ego and reason. You will know, perhaps, the master's voice in certain of these words. This contiguity is that which, the master says, 'permits a graphic chain to be adapted, on occasion in a linear fashion, to a spoken chain.' [11] Articulation. Writing articulates the interior, joining it, without precedence or antecedence, to the exterior. Writing is, in this sense, anacoluthon. Both Descartes and Kant are able to characterise themselves as not-followers because writing splits their selves. They can deny their following only because both versions of the self are interior, and, simultaneously, exterior to each other. But, in the text, the exterior crosses through to the interior along the conduit of the *ergo,* enabling them to become their own disciples. Writing accommodates the discipled self by virtue of this ergonomics.

9. Ergonomics of the soul

If indeed it is the technicity of writing that enables the Cartesian and Kantian foundings, then both founders might appear as disciples of that earlier disciple of both Christ and reason – Augustine. Augustine's writing of his own self, the *Confessions*, performs a prevenient version of self-division: ' . . . these two wills, one old, one new, one carnal, the other spiritual, contended with each other and disturbed my soul.' [12] Here, Augustine distinguishes between the temporal and the spatial modes of extension so that the 'old' and the 'new' contend, and the 'carnal' squares up to the 'spiritual'. Curiously, this suggests not only the contiguity of space and time in the unity of an experience, but the contiguity of two times and two spaces in the disunity of experience, the disunity of *disturbance* within another self – what Augustine calls the soul.

The soul seems to be an effect of the splitting of the temporal and the spatial, and of their discontiguity; it is necessitated as a textual figure of the observing consciousness. The soul performs the ergonomic function of accommodating the split temporality of old and new, and the split spatiality of carnal and spiritual. It is the appearance within the text of the technicity of writing – a term that appears as the disguised figure of the technical process by which a self is written. As such, it is what enables predication. Self-identity and self-division constitute the soul. If multiple Augustines produce ecstasy – *ek-stasis*, the standing outside of oneself – then the soul gathers together disparate selves, articulates them, joining and separating them in the same movement. It is the ergonomic function of the soul that enables confession – the writing of the self. But this ergonomics is a betrayal of the creed of self-diffraction or dissolution associated with Pauline conversion.

10. The (un)broken chain

The pattern is repeated. After Augustine comes Petrarch. Jill Robbins makes the observation that when Petrarch was converted in response to his reading of Augustine's *Confessions*, he failed to pass on to his brother the oracular words that might have brought him to a similar conversion:

> Petrarch, in denying his brother an oracle, in excluding him from conversion, brings to a halt the chain reaction his conversion could and should set off. Because of this distressing denial of fraternity and disregard of an Augustinian precedent of which he was well aware, Petrarch follows an example, yet does not become an example: *he follows and does not follow Augustine.*[13]

11. The most dangerous party member

Augustine's self splits around the event or process of conversion. Conversion, then, may be the experiential ground of anacoluthon. The autobiographical and doctrinal texts of that definitive model of conversion Saul/Paul, suggest that conversion is anacoluthic. His Christian subject is both continuous and discontinuous with its preconversion self: I and not I.

The Pauline text *is* anacoluthon: the point of cultural articulation, the double-jointed writing of a belated disciple. The persecutor became the disciple and performed his multiple anacolutha by articulating the breach between Jew and Greek, between gospel and epistle, between 'old' testament and 'new' testament, between the eye-witnesses and those who, like Paul himself, according to his own testimony, were 'born out of time'.

The most articulate and the most articulated of disciples, Paul inverts Judas, moving from betrayal to discipleship. But, as we have already seen, discipleship is itself betrayal. Paul breaches his trust, exceeds the *ipissima verba*, produces the Church Articulate, supplanting the founder with his own corpus. A belated, textual body of Christ. Paul becomes 'the most dangerous party member . . . provoking others to apostasy': the apostasy of discipleship, belatedness, and the heresy of articulation.

12. Coupling and uncoupling

For Slavoj Žižek, Christianity, in the person or text of Paul, performs a disjunction or uncoupling, in that it detaches the individual from the All, the subject from the cosmic order, allowing an individual 'immediate access to the universality (of nirvana, of the Holy Spirit . . .)'. In Christianity, one does not relate to the cosmos through one's 'place within the global social order', as in paganism, but on the basis of one's personal connection with the sotereological event:

> Christianity asserts as the highest act precisely what pagan wisdom condemns as the source of Evil, i.e. the gesture of *separation*, of drawing the line, of clinging to an element that disturbs the balance of All . . . . Christianity is the miraculous Event that disturbs the balance of the One-All, it is the violent intrusion of Difference that precisely throws off the rails the balanced circuit of the universe.[14]

Here, one follows Paul following Christ by means of a detachment: the joining is also a disjunction. But this hardly conforms to the logic of anacoluthon since it offers the possibility of a radical break, of an absolute discontinuity in which the old knows nothing of the new, nor the new of the old. If this were possible, anacoluthon would be an ancient trope of failed rhetoric.

The radical break appears to be possible in Žižek's rhetoric purely by virtue of Paul's insistence that in Christ one is a new creature: 'everything old has passed away; see everything has become new' (2 Cor. 5: 16–17). Žižek comments: 'The term "new creation" is tell-tale here, signalling the gesture of sublimation, of erasing the traces of one's past . . . and beginning afresh from a zero-point.'[15] We know, don't we, that this is never the case: everything old has never yet passed away. If nothing else proves it, language does. In fact, Paul's own text reminds of this in many ways, despite its contrary claims. Paul must rehearse his own past in order to prove that he is no longer Saul, and to give the weight of experience to his apostolic credentials. Yet, if he is not Saul, the rehearsal of the past becomes meaningless. There must be continuity for the discontinuity to make sense. Again, we might note that this is his *second* letter to the Corinthians, as the members of that congregation are still making the same mistakes that the first epistle addressed, to the extent that Paul fears he might have to begin again from scratch by repeating the story that legitimates his authority: 'Do we begin again to commend ourselves?' (2 Cor. 3:1). If 'everything old has passed away,' what is it in the Corinthian church that requires reiteration of the fact? Why would such a statement even need to be made if there were not an apparent continuity that required denying? Just so, Žižek's 'Christian uncoupling' must also be a coupling in that the 'difference' that marks the Christian event can only be recognised as such inasmuch as it is continuous with the order that it also disrupts.

13. The orthodox

As Plato, Aristotle, Paul, Augustine, Descartes and Kant all reveal, whatever the nature of our following, whoever we look to as founder, we are all heretics. There is nothing more orthodox.

14. The breach

Articulation is the breach: the contiguity of space and time in the unity of an experience, their joining and their difference. But it is also the trace of a disturbance: the scarring discomfort that predicates discipleship. So, once more unto the breach. If there are many reasons to return to it now, not least among them will be a troubling suspicion that its double meaning has been lost, or, at least, occluded by advocations of discontinuity that have severed (without joining) epistemes, phrase regimes, metanarratives, discourses: those descriptions of postmodernity that seem to accommodate comfortably various modes of cognitive dehiscence. Could the news of cognitive dehiscence ever reach us without invisible synapses to reticulate the seeming void, joining/not joining one epoch with another, one discourse, or discipline with another, one text with another? How did we come to hear of the breach? From what vantage point were we able to recognise its outline, trace its topography, or speak of its threatening promise?

15. Kiss

The gaps between these thoughts may open onto, or allow movement towards, many discursive spaces, in which unfold questions of auto/biography, historicity, influence, subjectivity, the connectivity constitutive of the institution, or other concerns which hinge upon the following/not following of one text, discourse, period, or self, and another. With inescapable open-endedness, irresistible freedom, anacoluthon invites speculation on what kind of discursive connections might be made. In doing so, it loosens the fabric of a (male) tradition which has defined itself by both (gender) identity and (individual) isolation. Here, the disruptive work of an ancient, yet largely unexplored trope, brings to light the continuities/discontinuities of what appears to be a history, and subjects them, at every turn, to the hidden, unmasterable work of the space of gestation in which all connections are made and unmade.

These turns about the hinge of anacoluthon are outlined in the hope that something may be found or founded to articulate the possibility of connection between solitary/solidary finders, researchers, founders of new texts. What began in the aftermath of a kiss – the physical articulation of a mouth touching the skin of another, concludes with this gesture towards the work of others, who, like its author, come after one master or another, who live in the epoch of AD – Anno Domini / After Derrida. Of course, one should always beware such gestures of recognition: the familiar approach, the kiss of greeting.

Father Away in the Forest of Books

Before I was born I was female and named for a tree. My mother wanted a girl, and throughout my gestation I was called Hazel in anticipation (after a friend of my mother's, who was the sister of the author Patricia St John).

I live in a village called Hengoed which means 'old wood'. I moved here from another village called Gelligaer, meaning 'copse fort'.

Today I work at the University of Glamorgan, the main campus of which institution is situated in a village called Trefforest (Forest Town) – contiguous with the town of Pontypridd. The building in which my department is located is called 'Forest Hall'.

Tree – copse – wood – forest. The plot thickens.

1. Into the Forest

> Midway life's journey I was made aware
> That I had strayed into a dark forest,
> And the right path appeared not anywhere
> Dante, *Inferno*, Canto I, ll.1–3, trans. Laurence Binyon

Dante's familiar mid-life crisis was a matter of forests and paths. By the time one reaches middle life, one has become only too aware that the world is indeed forest-like – an entangled business woven from too many possibilities for a single lifetime, overgrown with infinite inextricably interwoven complications. Faced with the recognition that the path we are on may not, thus far, have afforded us the richest experience, the most exotic views, the optimum number of opportunities for 'burning with a hard gem-like flame,' as Walter Pater famously put it, we may well sigh for a Virgil to lead us. But the sigh of the middle-aged academic involved in the professional study of literature will conjure not Virgil but Shakespeare. For, as we all know, to be engaged in literary criticism in the English-speaking world is to live with the constant presence of that literary shade.

Unlike Dante's Virgil, our Shakespeare is unlikely to lead us truly through the circles of Hell, up the Mount of Purgatory and into the dull, but secure, presence of God. But there was a time when *King Lear* was read in just this way – as a story of spiritual redemption; the king lost on the heath, we were told, ascends an inner *purgatorio*. Of course, we have long been disenchanted with such allegories and their disembodied figures. Now we notice not Lear's inward transfiguration, but his damaged flesh, and the sheer physicality of Shakespeare's language kills the spirit and revivifies the letter. John Russell Brown puts it succinctly:

> In a way that was new to himself and almost unknown in the theatre of his time, Shakespeare constantly drew attention to what his hero undergoes in body as well as in mind, in his senses as well as his thoughts and feelings.[1]

This earthbound Lear, so far removed from his erstwhile avatar, returns us willy-nilly to bodies and letters, to the bodiliness of letters, reminding us in the process that the material conditions to which we have confined the tormented old man and his dead daughters, are the limits of our own critical practice. We are the heath. But the converse is also true: we know that Shakespeare will not lead us off the heath, or out of the forest, because he himself *is* the forest in which we are lost. Embodied as the story of his interpretation and reinterpretation, he is the materiality of language and the history of literature. By which I mean that to engage in the process of writing is always to lag behind Shakespeare.

To turn to Shakespeare, to turn onto or into Shakespeare, to return to Shakespeare, is, in the end, to acknowledge one's lostness, one's deep immersion without return in the forest of books. For it is to acknowledge the existence of many thousand pathways, none of which is quite our own. A path, after all, by definition, is a way already trodden. To write is to re-write. And to write about Shakespeare is to confront the problem of criticism in its most basic, most intractable form: what is yet to be said? Shakespeare is the critical conundrum writ large. Writ long. Writ every-bloody-where.

And *As You Like It* – that drama of exile and forest-dwelling – is a parable of criticism. At least, so it appears to a male, middle-aged critic on no particular career path, or disciplinary byway. It places us, like its characters, and like the character in a parable by Borges, in a forest of forking paths. It is a ludic text that messes gleefully with our strategies of containment. By which I do not mean that it encourages us to play the usual critical games with it by, more or less, sanctioning our love of resistance to closure in terms of gender, class, ideology, identity, genre and so on. What I mean is that as a familiar Shakespearean comedy its interpretative potential is so overdetermined as to make such games seem stale and unproductive, and its particular interweaving of social, historical, cultural and literary discourses is so dense as to make any specific approach outrageously tendentious. No one path ameliorates the sense of anomie, loss, or bewilderment occasioned by the sheer entanglement of its notional structures. We cannot, for example, undress the layered figures of gender representation without pursuing those genetico-ideological wraiths entwined under the tired banner of 'subjectivity'; in turn, we cannot explore the play's playing with subjectivity unless we address the issues of inheritance – the nice historical specificities involved in the system of property and its passing between generations; how can we unpick the problem of primogeniture unless we also engage with the conditions of production that plays rich against poor, the courtly against the rural? In order to elucidate the distribution of power and wealth, interwoven as it is with the division between the rural and the urban, we have to map the generic implications of the pastoral mode and its satirical treatment in Shakespeare's comedy, but that is difficult unless we can unpick the extent to which the classical idea of the golden age is complementary to, or at odds with, the Edenic myth that resounds throughout the play. Of course, to address the biblical mythology is always to raise questions of . . . well . . . of gender. This is the danger inherent in entering the forest – you end up going round in circles.

We might see *As You Like It* as a particularly puzzling maze that invites the critic in with the suggestion that such a dense reticulation of cultural, historical, literary and linguistic strands, if it cannot be unravelled, can at least offer us the opportunity to trace through the weft a less noticed thread. Or, to go back to the path metaphor: we may not break a path, but we can (perhaps) plan an interesting route, or find a pleasing diversion. One way or another, we must get de Boys through the densely woven plain of Arden and back to town, but there is more than one route, and all roads lead to roaming.

My way – which is many ways – is the way of the fathers: dead fathers, exiled fathers, adoptive fathers, spiritual fathers, fathers who are brothers, brothers who are fathers, fathers who are uncles, servants who are fathers. I want to follow this avenue of thought, and its offshoot cul-de-sacs, for many reasons. Firstly, because I am thinking of criticism as a prodigal discourse, and this involves the attempts we make to leave behind our disciplinary and intellectual forebears.

The second reason is that the characters in *As You Like It,* especially in the opening scenes, seem to speak incessantly about fathers: Rosalind remembers 'a banished father' (I. ii. 4), and, just a few lines further on, Celia expresses the wish that they had the same father; later in the same scene, Le Beau tells Rosalind and Celia of the 'poor old man' who is father to three sons physically broken by combat with Charles the wrestler; the usurping Duke tells Orlando that he could wish him the son of a different father (I. ii. 212–13); Rosalind tells Celia that her father loved Orlando's father (I. iii. 29); when Rosalind is banished, it is because she is her father's daughter (I. iii. 56). And so it goes on. There are banished fathers, loved fathers, hated fathers, dead fathers, bereaved fathers, missed fathers, imaginary fathers.

Thirdly, the play alludes to the story of the prodigal son, specifically in relation to the problem of the patriarchal inheritance and how one relates to the previous generation.

Fourthly, because Shakespeare is our cultural father: the canon's paterfamilias, from whom I have tried to run away, and to whom I now return. Though not penitently.

Even now, as I close with the theme of fatherhood, the routes are multiple: I could pursue Harold Bloom for whom Shakespeare is not only the 'Center of the Canon' – the father of English literature, but also the inventor of the human – a Frankenstein-like parthenogenitor of our sense of ourselves. I could join hands with Gilbert and Gubar in exploring the implications of a literary and cultural patriarchy in which Shakespeare is a key figure. I could engage with Louis Montrose who traces the ways in which the tradition of primogeniture (a mode of construing father–son relationships) shapes the dramatic action of *As You Like It*. I could dialogue with Steven Marx in his exploration of the relationship between Shakespeare and that other great fathering text of the early modern age – the King James Bible. Of course, I deny that they have done what I want to do. I like to think that some kind of parthenogenesis is happening here, that this is a self-fathering text, but I know better. Where I desire to follow none, I shall probably follow all. I shall also be following those I do not even know; the absent father and the invisible mother, be they dead, exiled, disputed, or unknown, they have their monuments in all texts.

My method, then, will be to raise fingerposts, to point the way, like a father might, marking where I think we may usefully turn. Think that you are faced with a prodigal signpost that has many moving fingers.

2. Librosclerosis

It begins with a kind of disavowal born of a moment of librosclerosis in which the weight of books presses down on the student, paralysing the brain, making it impossible to read. For Shakespeare, I have to confess, is one of the fathers from whom I have run. My flight occurred when, as an undergraduate, I was required to write an essay on *Hamlet*. I went to the library to find some critical works with which to engage, only to find myself confronted with the terrifying stretches of crammed shelving devoted to the over-examined tragedies, histories and comedies of the onlie begetter. In that moment, I sensed that Shakespeare was not just another writer. Other authors had half a shelf, a whole shelf, maybe even two, devoted to them, but no single one of them had more than a fraction of the space devoted to Shakespeare. The difference seemed not merely quantitative; it was onto-logical. I had read and written about Sterne, Fielding, Austen, George Eliot, Dickens, and Hopkins, with no fear or compunction. But Shakespeare . . . this was scripture, holy writ, the canonical centre (as Bloom would have it) of all English literary creation and critique. To do Shakespeare was to be. But, in the face of all this published opinion, this history of considered response, this aged pre-eminence, it was also to acquiesce, to acknowledge one's belonging, and to be at home within the established order. It was to accept, I imagined, the judgement of the politicians, imperialists, capital-ists, rulers, authorities, principalities, powers, patriarchs, Tories, Oxbridge professors, elitists, bourgeois art-fanciers, London-based theatre-monkeys, the BBC, the English at large, that Shakespeare, the Bard, the iconic word-smith, was a demigod and the father of our literary, linguistic, and cultural heritage. And this I did not want either to accept or to acknowledge. He seemed to stand for everything that I was not, and for everything that I desired to resist, or to escape – to be, as Terry Eagleton puts it: 'this conser-vative patriarch . . . '[2] I fled in a kind of defiant panic. I went home and wrote a deconstructive response to *Hamlet*, drawing on no critical texts at all. I appended to the essay a note for my tutor, explaining that the infinite variety of Shakespeare scholarship had given me pause, and that I under-stood discretion to be the better part of valour. It worked. And I learned that not reading Shakespeare criticism was a good thing.Ever since, I have kept Shakespeare at arm's length for four reasons, each one a source of graphosclerosis: the anxieties of ignorance, of indolence, of influence and of impotence. How could I hope to know enough? How could I hope to read enough? How could I hope to write anything approaching the new, or even the unfamiliar? Could I find anything to say at all? Today, by which I mean – here, at the scene of writing – I will attempt some kind of a return. Of necessity really, since I now have to teach Shakespeare and time is too short for me not to write about what I am also teaching. So, I will obey the command of Stephano in *The Tempest*, to 'kiss the book', remembering that a kiss is not unequivocally a sign of love, devotion, or respect, but also of betrayal, disposal and perdition. It is a kind of escape too – a farewell: a way out for cowards, heroes, and zealots.

3. The Forest of Books

The forest is also a library that, left untreated, can reproduce something of the sclerotic immobilisation induced by shelves of critical works. When we first hear of it, in the words of Charles the wrestler – he who cripples and immobilises until 'there is little hope of life' in his victims (I. ii. 118–19) – it is already bookish: mediated by folkloric, pastoral, and classical allusions:

> Oliver
> Where will the old Duke live?
>
> **Charles**
> They say he is already in the Forest of Arden,
> and a many merry men with him; and there they live
> like the old Robin Hood of England: they say many
> young gentlemen flock to him every day, and fleet the
> time carelessly as they did in the golden world.
> (I. i. 108–12)

Even its name – the Forest of Arden – has the multiple possibilities of poetic usage: it is Arden in Warwickshire, Ardennes in France, and even the Garden of Eden (replete, as many have noted, with an Adam, a snake, and a tree). It also evokes Shakespeare's own family tree of course, the name of his maternal line, a trace of the invisible mother.

When the play actually takes us into the forest at the start of the second act, the first speech set in the sylvan scene accentuates the literary effect:

> And this our life, exempt from public haunt,
> Finds tongues in trees, books in the running brooks,
> Sermons in stones, and good in everything.
> (II. i. 15–17)

The Duke's words evoke the traditional image of the Book of Nature, but they also feed into a more pervasive sense that this is a book without covers, without limits, that what we are confronted by is not so much the Book of

Nature as its textuality. For what the forest reveals is not sermons so much as satires: the satirical response of Rosalind to the conventional love of the shepherds Silvius and Phebe, the rhetorical bullying of Corin by Touchstone, and the cynical detachment of Jaques that turns the freedom of the forest into 'as large a charter as the wind to blow on whom [he] please[s]' (II. vii. 48–9). He becomes the complete satirist, even, at one point, offering a Sidney-like defence of the genre (II. vii. 70–87).

Given the layered literariness of the forest, it is not surprising to find Orlando turning poet among the trees, nor to see him using them as his materials:

> Hang there, my verse, in witness of my love;
> And thou, thrice crown'ed queen of night, survey
> With thy chaste eye, from thy pale sphere above,
> Thy huntress' name that my full life doth sway.
> O Rosalind, these trees shall be my books,
> And in their bark my thoughts I'll character,
> That every eye which in this forest looks
> Shall see thy virtue witnessed everywhere.
> Run, run, Orlando, carve on every tree
> The fair, the chaste, the unexpressive she.
>
> (III. ii. 1–10)

Here the Duke's idea of nature speaking, of trees with tongues, stones delivering sermons, brooks writing books, is reversed by the image of a language *imposed* upon nature. Michael Mangan makes some telling observations:

> The trees in the Forest of Arden bear poems, not fruit (or 'bad fruit' as Touchstone calls them); their leaves are leaves of paper . . . . Orlando now intends to make the trees his books . . . . Meanwhile the thoughts which he articulates are themselves not couched in 'natural' language, but in the language of poetry. His speech is constructed with a formal rhyme-scheme which resembles that of the Elizabethan sonnet, rhyming ABAB CDCD EE; his apostrophe to the moon ('thrice crown'ed queen of night') is purely conventional, a cliché of Elizabethan love poetry.
>
> Just as Orlando decorates (or litters?) the forest with his poetic outpourings, so the play, set in this 'natural' world of the Forest of Arden, is permeated by the various languages of Elizabethan poetry.[3]

Orlando's reversal of the Duke's perception closes the system in on itself so that the forest writes only as it is written, and is written only as it writes.

The forest is a forest of poems, poetic conventions, multiple possibilities, interpretative pathways.

The problem of fathers and of how to be (or not to be) next in line is what brings us here, what makes of us runaways in Arcadia, looking for a path among the books.

4. My Father's Spirit

It will become clear that the runaway, whether a coward, a hero, or a zealot, is not always or necessarily a rebel to the will of the father; at least, not in any straightforward way. For the will of the father is a house divided against itself; like all manifestations of power, it is internally riven. Shakespeare's famous father figures show us this, whether we think of Lear's division of his kingdom that leads to the self-division of his madness, or of the way in which the ghost of his dead father divides Hamlet between revenge and self-immolation. In the latter case, it becomes evident that the internalised voice of the father is a participant in the dialogue of the self in its search for autonomy and a place of its own in contradistinction with the father as predecessor, role model, begetter. Such is clearly the case, too, in Shakespeare's version of the prodigal, *As You Like It*. These are the words of Orlando to his elder brother, Oliver, in the opening scene:

> My father charged you in his will to give me good education: you have trained me like a peasant, obscuring and hiding from me all gentleman-like qualities. The spirit of my father grows strong in me, and I will no longer endure it. Therefore allow me such exercises as may become a gentleman, or give me the poor allottery my father left me by testament; with that I will go buy my fortunes. (I. i. 62–9)

The spirit of the father in this instance seems to be an inner voice that Shakespeare would later actually put onstage in the form of the ghost of the dead king in *Hamlet*. Paul Yachnin writes of the parallel between Orlando and Hamlet:

> For these characters (and we can add Prince Hal too), inwardness arises because of the introspection they undertake in order to authenticate both their spiritual bond with their fathers and their legitimacy as their fathers' sons. Orlando and especially Hamlet and Hal are avatars of inwardness because they are given to bouts of self-inspection in their keen investigation of their own bloodlines.[4]

The bloodline and the inwardness may be closely connected, but they are also in conflict. Hamlet's struggle with the voice of his dead father kills him in the end. That's tragedy. The comic version is far darker. It offers no clear, definable conflict that might be resolved by the demise of any single figure. Rather, it allows the conflict insidiously to seep out in every direction, so that the relationship between son and father infects those between brothers (Orlando and Oliver, Duke Senior and Duke Frederick), between father and daughter (Duke Senior and Rosalind, Duke Frederick and Celia), between uncle and niece (Duke Frederick and Rosalind), and between cousins (Rosalind and Celia), as well as between male and female, feminine and masculine. The whole family gets involved. All except the mother, that is. Prodigals are notoriously motherless.

Early on in the opening scene, Orlando makes his relation to the parable of the prodigal son quite clear: 'Shall I keep your hogs and eat husks with them? What prodigal portion have I spent, that I should come to such penury?' Despite these direct allusions to the parable, there are very obvious differences between the situations described. In Shakespeare's tale, the father is already dead, and it is to his elder brother that Orlando has to appeal for his 'allottery'. The elder brother replaces the father as the figure of authority, inheriting his position and wealth, but using it rather differently. But Orlando is said by the servant (Adam) to be the 'memory of Old Sir Rowland' (II. ii. 2–3) – the living image of the dead father – and he himself claims to be motivated by his father's 'spirit'. So, the father is divided between the power and wealth that reside with the elder brother, and the image and 'spirit' that imbue Orlando with the desire and courage to resist the status quo. Furthermore, when the prodigal son returns to his father, he does so on the basis that he is willing to accept the status of a servant, already having had to become accustomed to keeping hogs and eating husks with them. Shakespeare's scenario inverts this situation: Orlando is *unwilling* to be a servant, and his offer to dine with the livestock is sarcastic. He denies being a prodigal, but feels that he is being forced into the role, and so, ironically, he embraces the role by running away. That act dramatises the father's inner division.

Thus when Louis Montrose observes that the relationship between brother and brother becomes identified with the relationship between father and son, he is nearly right; nearly, but not quite. [5] And here, he is not altogether true to his own best insight. For he argues that the opposition between subversion and containment that divides materialist doctrines between Foucauldian new historicists and other cultural materialists, is fruitless and reductive. The new historicists typically contend that subversion is more or less impossible, since we read as 'subversive' whatever belongs to, confirms, or conforms with, our own sense of the way things should be, over against how they appear to have been at some moment in history. Thus subversion comes to mean something akin to its opposite: the reinforcement of our own values through the political reading of works from the past. The contrary case is argued by cultural materialists who see resistance to power, or at least, propensities to question or problematise ideological formations, everywhere at work in cultural productions. Montrose argues that ideology is highly variegated, and that power does not gather or circulate in predictable, stable or undifferentiated forms. [6] Power can thus be seen to be both self-subverting, and dependent upon subversion for its own maintenance. This is only paradoxical if power is monolithic; if, as Montrose contends, it is riven, diverse, uneven in its distribution and effects, then its elements may well be in competition or even conflict. One can see just this kind of internal rivenness in the roles of fathers in *As You Like It,* especially in that father Montrose allows to pass unproblematically into the person of his elder son.

5. Doublings

This problem between brothers – each claiming the place of the father – is, like so many things in *As You Like It*, doubled. Before Oliver and Orlando have their spat, the Duke has already been usurped by his younger brother in a conflict still awaiting resolution. The play opens with the split between Orlando and Oliver coming to crisis. It opens, in other words, with a double mitosis: this moment splits the father's heritage, doubling the division of Duke versus Duke. From there the doubling and inversions in *As You Like It* spread like a virus: there are two settings, two daughters, two dukes, two Olivers, two Jaques, two shepherds, two servants; Arden in Warwickshire is also Ardennes in France (or Belgium), Touchstone is also 'the clown', Rosalind is also Ganymede, Celia is also Aliena; the name de Boys has a French meaning ('of the woods') and an English connotation ('about boys'); then there are the contrasting pairings of the shepherdess (Phebe) with the country woman uninflected by pastoral idealisation (Audrey), and the country youth (William) with the shepherd (Silvius). Furthermore, as Montrose points out: when Orlando marries Rosalind, and Oliver marries Celia, the younger brother marries the daughter of an elder brother, and the elder brother marries the daughter of a younger brother, in a chiasmus that crosses their destinies: for Orlando will leave the forest to become the nobleman, heir of the duke, while Oliver will resign his estates, and 'live and die a shepherd' (V. ii. 10–12).[7]

It would take a keen structuralist, or some fancy algebra, to tabulate, or calculate, the interplay between all of these couplings. I am content to admit that they make me nervous. I also confess to a worry about the fact that Orlando and Oliver have another brother called Jaques, who is away at school. He complicates the problem of what happens between fathers and sons, and upsets my plans. Happily, the play keeps the scholar at bay for most of the time, leaving me free (for now) to observe timidly that in doubling the action, the characters and the setting, as well as in varying the key relationships within the family structures, the play allows parallels and disjunctions that open windows on complex relations of power that are distributed across a range of cultural divides: town and country, social classes, familial relations, generation gaps, gender, versions of the self. It is clear that power is not monolithic in *As You Like It*; rather it is invested in a range of interrelated formations, and negotiated on multiple, criss-crossing fronts. The critical possibilities are legion: patriarchy and the patronymic tradition are destabilised, gender and sexuality are neither fixed nor securely embedded in the human organism, the real and the ideal do not remain comfortably discrete, class structures fail to contain the contrary energies of rivals within the system of privilege, selfhood is fluid, multiple, negotiable. This is the forest of forking paths. Since no critical discourse can pursue every path, and in choosing one path among many, the critic deforms the story, deserts it, and strikes out in search of distinction, anything can happen here. Go which way you please.

6. Servant Power

It has pleased most critics to avoid the servants. Every reading of the parable of the prodigal son that I have encountered obliterates the role of the servants, despite the fact that they are present in the tale as crucial actors in the unfolding of the drama, and their roles relate them closely to that played by the father. The voice of the father in the prodigal's mind – the voice that urges return – is inseparable from the role of the servants who do the father's bidding. As we have seen, the prodigal's inner dialogue posits his own superiority over the servants as a reason to return: 'How many hired servants of my father's have bread enough and to spare, and I perish with hunger? I will arise and go to my father' (Luke 15:17–18). The servants act not only as instructive exempla of domestic comfort and security, but also as alternative ways of constructing the son's identity: they are possible role models for what the son may become. For he ponders the option of returning not as a son, but as a servant: 'I will arise and go to my father, and will say unto him,

Father, I have sinned against heaven, and before thee, And am no more worthy to be called thy son: make me as one of thy hired servants' (Luke 15:18–19). Here, the father has actually been displaced by the servants in the son's mind; he imagines becoming like them rather than like his father.

The prodigal son's consideration of the possibilities for stepping out of the self-replicating system of generational succession is echoed in *As You Like It* by the actions and assertions of various characters. Most obviously, Rosalind adopts not only a change of gender in becoming Ganymede, but also a change of social status or rank: she specifically notes that this role is one of a servant: 'I'll have no worse a name than Jove's own page, And therefore look you call me Ganymede' (I. iii. 122–3). In response, Celia adopts the name Aliena, suggesting, if not servitude exactly, at least a stepping out of the familial structure, a distancing, estranging, or alienation from the domestic sphere. Jaques, whose actual social position has been debated, expresses a desire to change his station: 'O that I were a fool! I am ambitious for a motley coat' (II. vii. 42–3). Ambition has somehow gone into reverse as the characters move out from the court and its static structures, into the social entanglements of the forest.

These devices and desires that extricate the characters from the familiar patterns of power probably parody what, in another context, Regenia Gagnier refers to as 'status anxiety' – the worry that the burgeoning economics of capitalism in early modern England would destabilise social hierarchies.[8] But they also serve to highlight the diffraction of patriarchal power by desire. An order of things has begun to unravel in the play, and even individual identity has loosened, slipped its moorings in the patronymic tradition. The changing of names and stations is a prodigal procedure by which fathers are given the slip. Names dissolve as the self-fashioning ethos of the courtier escapes the confines of the court and slips out into the woods for a bit of a lark. For this woodland beyond the walls is not quite the same kind of place as that hinterland in which the mad King Lear would discover the bare forked animal beneath the façade of culture; it is little more than a pretence, but it is dangerously close to the heath because it lies in that gap between generations.

Peter Barry (*aside*)
The traditional distinction between heath and forest in Shakespeare is that you lose yourself in the forest and find yourself on the heath.

Kevin Mills
My perception of their proximity goes along with a suspicion that losing yourself and finding yourself are not necessarily different things. When the

prodigal comes to himself it is only inasmuch as he knows his own lostness. It is in the severance or discontinuity – that allows him to identify with the servants rather than the father – that he is rejoined to his self-consciousness.

The forest games are a masque, a playful evocation of Robin Hood's Sherwood, a country retreat. But the role infects the actors; the forest creeps into the court; there will not be a full return to the *status quo ante*; there will be a realignment of fatherly relations. Oliver will actually ask his *younger* brother's consent to marry, while Orlando will inherit the father's estate when Oliver goes off to 'live and die a shepherd.' Oliver, then, will take on the pastoral life, will become the feeder of livestock that Orlando refused to be. Orlando will become adopted son and heir to the Duke, outbidding his father's and his brother's erstwhile social status, more than realising his ambition to match his father's spirit, though the line of inheritance has been distorted or even derailed, in order to produce this outcome. Celia will lose her father to the religious life, effectively exchanging places with Rosalind under the care of an uncle.

Shakespeare, then, seems to have woven into the fabric of *As You Like It,* all kinds of variations on the theme of the prodigal son's putative self-reinvention as a servant during his sojourn in the countryside, away from the hierarchy of the patriarchal home. In Shakespeare's version, there is no return to the order that has been left behind; but there are many possible outcomes of the rupture in the social texture caused by running away. The inverted ambition of those who trade down – the masters who envy their servants some kind of self-realisation not available within the stations of gentility – opens the walls and subverts the boundaries. But the contrary case has a similar outcome, in that the one character to specifically allude in his speeches to the parable – Orlando – is adamant that *he will not* accept the status of servant in his father's / brother's house. And it is just this vehement rejection of the role of servant that leads to the ensuing crisis, and to his sojourn in the forest in close proximity to the lives of the very workers whose lot he has disdained. Not only does he find himself among shepherds, but he has been brought to this place thanks to both the care and the money of a servant.

Orlando's flight to the Forest of Arden is occasioned by the warning administered by Adam that Oliver 'means To burn the lodging where you use to lie, And you within it . . . this house is but a butchery; Abhor it, fear it, do not enter it' (II. iii. 22–4). At this point, as if to remind us that his presence has implications for father/son relationships Adam's language becomes antithetical on the issue: 'Your brother – no, no brother – yet the son – Yet not the son, I will not call him son Of him I was about to call his father' (II. iii. 19–21). It is as if a combination of age, disapproval, and, it has to be said, a degree of fatherly feeling, combine to deform family relations in Adam's mind. This deformation is intensified in what follows. On being told not to enter the house, Orlando objects that he has nowhere else to go, and oddly, given that he is talking to a servant rather than to a parent, sarcastically asks whether Adam would have him become a beggar or a thief 'on the common road'. In another unlikely twist, Adam's response is to offer him money: 'I have five hundred crowns, The thrifty hire I saved under your father . . . Here is the gold; All this I give you' (II. iii. 38–46). Orlando, the despiser of the servant's role, becomes the inheritor of a servant's life savings.

Following on from the brother/not brother, son/not son speech, in which familial doubts are sown and paternity destabilised by a servant, the scene takes on something of the tone of the exchange between the father and son in the parable: the son receiving money for his journey from the father. But the sense is twisted away from paternal devotion by the fact that Adam's words actually evoke another aspect of the parable when he adds 'Let me be your servant'. In the parable, these are the words of son to father. The confusion of servant, father, and son, or at least the partial blending of the roles in the play, seems to me to comment on, or even to be an interpretation of, the parable in which the will of the father cannot be extricated from the role of the servants, and the role of servants is part of the inner dialogue of the son.

We might also recall that at the beginning of the play Adam is present as the issue of fatherhood is raised and discussed. When Orlando first mentions his father's spirit within him, it is to Adam. When, subsequently, he argues with Oliver and insists that he has as much of his father in him as does his elder brother, Adam is standing by watching like some kind of presiding genius. Again, it is Adam who describes Orlando as the image of his father – the 'memory of old Sir Rowland'. But if Adam is a kind of surrogate father to Orlando, the arrangement seems temporary, as Montrose observes:

> Adam's paternity is only a phase in the reconstitution of Orlando's social identity. In the process of revealing his lineage to the old Duke, Orlando exchanges the father-surrogate who was his father's own servant for the father-surrogate who was his father's own lord . . . The living son replaces his dead father in the affections of their lord. The Duke, who has no natural son, assumes the role of Orlando's patron, his social father . . . Orlando's previous paternal benefactor has been supplanted: Adam neither speaks nor is mentioned again.[9]

Sadly, I think Montrose is right. The power of servants is not great. The debt to the servant is never repaid. He remains the unsung facilitator of the piece, his money and his service taken and forgotten. His purpose is merely instrumental in the rich man's progress. It is clear from both Adam's own testimony, and from that of Corin, that the landless, estate-less workers could expect little from their masters: Adam expects an 'unregarded age in corners thrown', and Corin, the hired shepherd, speaks of a 'master of a churlish disposition,' of his own poverty, and – in another echo of the parable of the prodigal son – a rustic home where there is no food to be found (Act 3, sc. 4).

7. All My Fathers

Fathers, as Shakespeare was clearly aware, have a habit of coming back; they haunt you. Thus it is that Orlando has four fathers: one dead before the play begins; the elder brother who inherits the paternal wealth and power and who treats Orlando like a bastard son; Adam, who shields him and sets him on an upward path; and the Duke, who adopts him and makes him rich and powerful. This is almost a parable of fatherhood in all its guises. It can have been no accident that the servant who enables Orlando's escape, who in effect saves his life, bears the name of the primal biblical father. Perhaps, then, Adam does not disappear after all, but is, spirit-like, translated into other forms. He is the archetypal father whose most vital, nurturing, enabling incarnation is in the form of a servant. I choose to think so because I once had a father who had been both a shepherd and a pastor, and because I am a father with little to bequeath. I read in the interests not of the law, but of the lore, of the father.

Orlando's many-fatheredness illustrates the way in which the self emerges as the product of the self-maintaining self-subversion of authority. For his father figures are not united in power, desire, status, love, nor even life. All are at odds. Orlando is the scene of their intersection, of their conflict, coalescence and violence. He is the knot in the divergent cords, a point of convergence and divergence. This is significant, for as Montrose points out (forgive me for returning once again to Montrose, but I have so little at my command, and this essay serves so well), Orlando is a young man; he is on the cusp of manhood, and in the process of self-definition:

> Orlando's youth is referred to by himself and by others some two dozen times in the first two scenes: he is young; a boy; a youth; the youngest son; a younger brother; a young fellow; a young gallant; a young man; a young

gentleman . . . The youthful members of an Elizabethan household . . . were all supposed to be kept under strict patriarchal control.[10]

Clearly, young Orlando is not under control. He resists control. He resists control not in his own name, but, paradoxically, in the name of the father who is dead, and who yet lives on. This is what it means to be a youth in search of oneself: to follow and not to follow the father: to resist the law of the father as the father once resisted the law and then came to be the law. This is the lore of the father: the story of the prodigal son.

It is perhaps for reasons such as these that Orlando's character never quite fixes. Even at the end of the play he seems like a barely known quantity, and the final scene offers us little opportunity to improve our knowledge of him. He is overshadowed by the wit of Touchstone, Jaques, and, most particularly, Rosalind, by comparison with whom he remains colourless. Here there is another of the twists or reversals that complicate the surface of the play. While Rosalind appears in disguise, her character is never in doubt; Orlando never appears in disguise, yet his character is fluid and uncertain. We see him in several very different roles, each one a kind of early-modern masculine archetype: the macho wrestler, stripped to the waist, and physically impressive; the courtly lover addressing poems to his lady, hopeless of requital; the knight errant at large in the dangerous forest; Robin Hood, taking food from the rich at the point of a sword to feed the poor; the prodigal son – hungry, desperate and down on his luck: 'the thorny point of bare distress' having taken from him 'the show of smooth civility' (II. vii. ll.95–7); the heroic fighter who risks his life to save a brother. Something of Orlando's multiplicity appears when, in one exchange with Rosalind, Celia describes his appearance in series of diverse images: 'I found him under a tree like a dropped acorn . . . stretched along like a wounded knight . . . furnished like a hunter' (III. ii. ll. 327–38). This Protean male thus demonstrates, or shows the effects of, the multiplicity of fatherhood – the rivenness that makes it impossible not to resist. And impossible to resist.

8. Convergence

Rosalind's resistance is more straightforward, at least in the sense that she has no siblings to complicate the lines of descent. Her flight from power is from her uncle, the usurping duke; she is a prodigal niece. But it is noticeable that although she follows him into exile she does not find, or even seem interested in finding, her father, for most of the play. She is untroubled by the paternal spirit that drives Orlando, freely adapting herself to a male role, fathering herself in the forest in a way that Orlando cannot do. But Rosalind's name, since it is almost an anagram of 'is Orlando', suggests that her role is, in certain respects, very much akin to his, at least in the sense that both are runaways whose relationship to the previous generation has become in some way problematical: both Rosalind and Orlando are figures of generational and familial disjunction: they both follow and do not follow their forebears. In Orlando's case, his father's 'spirit' leads him to run away from a situation that his father's will (in both senses of that word) has created. This dichotomy of the father is reflected in the respective positions of the two sons, as well as in the multiplicity of Orlando's own relation to his father(s).

For Rosalind, estrangement from her father is the product of a prevenient power struggle between himself and his brother. That struggle not only inverts the elder brother / younger brother conflict that divides Orlando from Oliver, but also invests Rosalind's situation with peculiar power: her predicament represents the outcome of a sibling rivalry that is the inverse of the one in which she becomes embroiled thanks to her attachment to Orlando. She has, then, a kind of bridging function, without which there is no connection between the two stories of brotherly conflict. It is as if there is more than one version of the story running at once: just as in Luke 15, where the parables of loss and recovery frame one another. In *As You Like It* Rosalind is the point of articulation in the drama, being connected in more directions than anyone else in the play. She has exchanges with Celia, Touchstone, Le Beau, Duke Frederick, Orlando, Corin, Phebe, Silvius, Jaques, Oliver, Duke Senior, and makes the final connection by addressing the audience in the epilogue. If the pastoral love story can be called a subplot, then she also acts as the link between plot and subplot, in that she intervenes in the troubled courtship of Phebe and Silvius.

Again, in her relationship with Touchstone, her story connects the role of the servant with the process of escape. In an inversion of the relationship between Orlando and Adam, it is she who facilitates his absconding:

Rosalind
But, cousin, what if we assayed to steal
The clownish fool out of your father's court:
Would he not be a comfort to our travel?
Act 1, sc. 3, ll. 127–9

To take Touchstone is, here, to resist fatherly power and ownership; it is to steal from the father's estate. The servant appears as portable property in a way that contrasts sharply with the image of servant as father/provider in Adam's relationship with Orlando.

So Rosalind's story parallels Orlando's, but varies it, adding another version of the story of running away from home. In doing so, Rosalind will actually be moving, unknowingly, towards her exiled father. For her, escape is return. In the long run, this will also prove to be true for Orlando, since the forest episode will bring him back to wealth and status lost on his father's death, but this will happen only because Rosalind is there to connect Orlando with her father, the Duke.

9. Invisible Mother

You will have seen the signs: we could read in another direction. Orlando's name is derived from Rosalind's. That is to say, Orlando's name almost equates to Rosalind minus the 'is': he is not Rosalind; he is never quite equal to her. Who could be? He plays parts that never quite convince. He does well enough at wrestling, but that physical prowess is not quite matched by his poor efforts at poetry; his dependence upon Adam makes him seem like a useless and parasitic aristocrat; his less than impressive presence among the members of the court-in-exile in the forest makes him appear inferior to his peers; his inadequacy as a student in the art of wooing reveals his inferiority to Rosalind. If he is redeemed, it is by his improbable struggle with a lioness to save the life of his reprobate brother – an episode so baldly contrived as to appear deliberately to undercut any inferred heroism. Rosalind, by contrast, has an easy superiority; she is more than a match for each and every one of her many interlocutors.

We might say that Rosalind's superiority interferes with Orlando's difficult lineage. After all, she does seem to appropriate the play (after an opening that might lead the audience to take Orlando for its hero), much as Oliver has appropriated Orlando's share of the father's estate. This is compounded by the fact that Orlando's name, which should, by patronymic convention, be derived from his father's, could equally well be derived from Rosalind's. Here, too, Shakespeare has been playing with anagrammatical possibilities, for the father was Rowland. Orlando derives exactly as much from his father's name as he does from Rosalind's – Orland; all that's missing is the o. Which is nothing. So, not only is he divided between versions of his father and himself, but he is also divided between Rosalind and his father. And, indeed, in her male role, Rosalind becomes yet another kind of father to Orlando: she takes on the task of instructing him in love. Or is that a mother's role? Rosalind might also be imagined as a mother, albeit an invisible one – cloaked by the male role and the pseudonym. Her real name might be the patronymic; or the patronymic may be a corruption of her name. Orlando certainly appears to have no other mother. Stories of the prodigal always seem to reverse the fact that, throughout history, mother-hood is fact; paternity is fiction. This is what parable means: an untrue story that encodes male desire.

10. Self-Service

Servants appear in the space from which mothers are erased: Rosalind appears in the forest as Ganymede – cup-bearer to the father of the gods, taking on the role of mother and servant, making up for the failure of fathers to see beyond their power-struggles and their self-replicating instincts. In the parable of the prodigal son, the absence of the mother is compensated for by the servants who not only call the son home in his memory of their domestic comfort, but who also re-clothe him and feed him: 'But the father said to his servants, Bring forth the best robe, and put it on him; and put a ring on his hand, and shoes on his feet: and bring hither the fatted calf, and kill it; and let us eat, and be merry' (Luke 15:22–23). The 'but' with which this quotation begins, indicates the father's countering of his son's expression of willingness to be a servant: he will not be a servant; he will be served. Servants will mother him, re-enfold him within the home, see to his needs.

One could almost read Hegel into the texts at this point, were it not for the fact that the masters and slaves of his dialectic are curiously inhuman and unsexed creatures whose relation to mothers is (prodigally) unstated. What might be valuable in such an appeal is that the formation of the self is at issue in that philosophical discourse, as in this unphilosophical one. According to Hegel's *Phenomenology of Spirit*, self-consciousness is produced by the desire to reduce all exterior phenomena to objecthood, so that the self knows itself in contrast with what it is not. But this is a little difficult since recognition of self-consciousness also requires that an equally self-conscious being understands and admits parity between the two, and this threatens the dissymmetry crucial to the formation of self-consciousness. This is where mastery and slavery emerge: in the charged reciprocity of self-recognition, one self-consciousness is more equal than the other. The stronger consciousness becomes the master, the weaker the slave. Of course, this simply displaces the problem, since the master now objectifies the slave. Conversely, the master's self-recognition now depends upon the inferior self-consciousness of the slave, while the slave's self-consciousness is reinforced through labour because it produces objective, material signs of its existence in the world. The slave's self-consciousness thus transcends that of the master.[11]

The parable of the prodigal son reflects that crucial moment in the dialectical process when the master recognises his inferiority to the slave, as the son recognises that his inheritance has produced not freedom, but an abjection that makes his father's servants figures of envy. In this recognition, Luke says, the son 'came to himself' (Luke 15:17). Self-recognition emerges only when mastery has run its course, spent its inheritance, and acknowledged its own servitude. In *As You Like It* we can see the dialectic at work in Orlando's dependence upon Adam, in Rosalind's servant disguise, in Jaques' recognition of himself in the figure of the fool, in Oliver's conversion to shepherd.

The rivenness of power, especially in its relation to fatherhood and mastery (patriarchy we might say), that makes it impossible to resist and impossible not to resist, is constitutive of the self. The self resides in the detour that power takes through the forest on its way home, a detour that may actually be its home. At least, inasmuch as the parabolist, the philosopher and the playwright agree. When I say 'agree', I mean something like meeting in a peopled forest.

I I. *In Loco Parentis*

We never leave the forest. It ends here with rumours of change filtering through the trees. We hear of the usurping Duke's conversion in an encounter with 'an old religious man' – a spiritual father who never presents himself to us, but remains on 'the skirts of this wild wood'. News of the conversion is borne to us by a stranger called de Boys. He is the other Jaques – the one we do not know – the third son who could not be accounted for in my scheme; he is the scholar of the family entering the woods with a clear sense of direction, with news of a way out. Believe it or not. It is in this light that we hear of *our* Jaques' intention to join the 'convertite' in a religious life: the scholar's entrance is also the cue for the cynical satirist to leave, for his refusal to join in the celebration. So one Jaques is replaced by another; the pattern of usurpation is repeated even in the comic denouement.

We also hear speculation that 'true delights' await. There will be a party to celebrate somebody's return. But none of these things quite belong to us. They are projected beyond the temporal and spatial frames of the text and the stage. We are among those outside. Somebody will come out to look for us, but, unlike in the story of the prodigal, it will not be the father, at least not the father we expect. We presume that the stage direction, *exeunt all except Rosalind*, means that when she addresses the audience in the epilogue, de Boys are back in town. That includes the scholarly son who promised so much. But she remains here talking with us, drawing us, not into the party, but into the emptying forest; the town is far away and out of sight. Like Jaques, we have not joined in the closing dance, but neither have we followed him into the religious life. All our fathers have left us, even the spiritual ones, and in the forest we are addressed by the mother dressed as a father – the boy-woman-man-woman-boy making jokes about kissing men. Camping in the forest; that is where we make ourselves at home. For now, anyway.

• • •

Before I was born I was female and named for a tree.

The Elder Brother

What I resent is being part of a tradition. Tradition means never being forgiven. It started with Cain; the first villain was an elder brother – the killer of his younger sibling. Why did he do it? Because he was undermined by his little brother. Abel edged him out of God's favour and took his place in the sun. Isn't that also a kind of murder? But we remember Cain's crime rather than Abel's usurpation.

After a few generations, along came unchosen, unpromised, unwelcome Ishmael. He was older than his brother Isaac, and he was banished by his father (Abraham) from the family so that the younger brother could inherit wealth, divine favour and the all-important promise.

Then there was Esau – the elder brother and patsy to the scheming Jacob. Jacob stole not only his elder brother's birthright, but also his place in legend. He made out that God hated Esau because he was the elder brother, because he was careless of his inheritance, and because he was a 'hairy man'. Jacob made primogeniture the antithesis of true religion; he made it look as if God himself hated elder brothers. Worse than that: he passed on the prejudice by favouring his own youngest son, Joseph. You remember Joseph; he flaunted his sense of his own superiority, pouring out to his older brothers his self-aggrandising dreams in his disingenuous faux naivety. Then he managed to make himself feel and look like a victim when they – naturally enough to my mind – were so revolted by his swaggering sense of self-importance that they sold him as a slave to some travelling merchants. It was a tactical error, of course, not only because it made his fortune in an unforeseen way, but also because it served to legitimate his sense of grievance. It gave him the air of one who had made it against all odds, as if the dice had not been loaded in his favour from the start. And look what happened: Joseph's story became a myth – an archetypal narrative to be turned into novels, films, even bloody musicals for God's sake. And every time the story is retold there's another nail in the coffin of the bad old elder brother; another laurel wreath for junior.

It is bad enough that the patriarchs were a club of younger brothers who schemed to overthrow the law of primogeniture, but, to make things worse, the whole business was repeated in the story of King David. And there's another myth for you – the lost king sought and found, the marvellous child cloaked in obscurity, the chosen one disregarded by all except God, or Fate, or Providence, blissfully ignorant of his own destiny. David was the youngest son of his father, and, of course, he made sure that the chronicles of his life – that *he* commissioned – depicted him as the undervalued child, the hidden wonder – born too late, lost in the hills with his sheep, but secretly chosen by God to be the greatest king in his nation's history. And this miraculous overturning of patriarchal succession, we are led to believe, ran counter to the law of the human fathers. Counter to the law? What kind of deception is that? The law of primogeniture was invented to mask the hegemony of the younger brothers so that they could convince themselves, and others, that *they* were the prodigals, the rebels, the freedom fighters. That way resistance to their rule was made to seem like the politics of resentment – reactionary and conservative.

The stories are always interpreted in favour of the younger brothers precisely because they seem to be the underdogs. Underdogs with God on their side – *you* figure it out. They always claim to be living in the shadow of their elder brothers while their own penumbra creeps stealthily over the world. You see it everywhere – this tyranny of runts. It tells us that new is better than old, that youth is better than age, that the most recent is the most advanced; the younger, the more desirable. It is the law of progress – the built-in obsolescence of the object, of the style, of the process, and even of the soul. Supersession has become the self-concealing law by which we live. Call it progress, call it free-market economics, call it decadence – it is all the same. It is the mark of Cain.

Such a ruthlessly clever disguise – not to hide your own face, but to disfigure your brother's. You murder him by taking his place in the order of things and you brand *him* a killer in the process. You steal everything he has and banish him from his empty home – send him out naked on the roads, stricken with the injustice of the skies for punishment.

Memory is the worst injustice. It has no comparators. I remember that when we were boys, we knew the truth. I led and he followed. I was the hero of our little world. I discovered the music, the books, the clothes, the ideas, the politics, the in-crowd. I fashioned myself, and he came along in my wake, doing his best to understand the vibe and to belong with me, deriving his sense of himself from *my* modes of expression. Then we interwove our thoughts and became a tangle of shared sensibilities. I suppose that, eventually, he needed to unweave himself from the web of affinities by pulling apart the fabric of my life.

He paid his dues, he'll tell you. He lived the high life and paid for it with hunger, poverty and life in a pigsty. He got his hands dirty. He claims to have rejected the insulating effect of inherited wealth in favour of an engagement with raw life, conveniently forgetting his own idiotic frittering away of time and money, his expense of spirit in a waste of shame. He forgets, too, the extent to which he has always relied – and continues to rely – on the name and status he inherited.

Somewhere along the line he learned the trick of turning his hand-me-down clothes – trimmed to a boho chic – into a uniform, a badge of office. School of hard knocks and all that. Now he thinks his little rebellion has earned him his place as an unacknowledged legislator of the world – a subversive, subterranean influence. But, in fact, he rules with a rod of iron from behind that façade. You'll know his most powerful avatars: they are those men who live on their inheritance – who allow us to know that they were once prodigal sons who grew their hair, smoked dope, joined protest marches, played in rock bands – and who wear that past as a way of disguising their own lust for power. They are the guitar-playing prime ministers, the sax-playing presidents, the young, dressed-down, 'regular guys' who start illegal wars, bomb innocent civilians, promote their friends to high office, and manipulate the limbs of a dead democracy as if it yet had life.

If I do not feel for him an unmixed contempt, it is only because I still see myself in my brother, and because I know that what he has become is an expression of a shared inheritance.

Splitting the Aphorism

1. The Name that Binds

Although an aphorism might be a short, pithy maxim, or a brief statement of a principle, according to the *OED*, it derives its name neither from its pithiness nor from its brevity, but from its character as separate, bounded, enclosed, shut in. It is the paradox, if not the tragedy, of the aphorism that its enclosure is the limit of the thinker's attempts to escape from the constraints of critical discourse. Or, at least, this appears to be the case in the work of the pioneer, Nietzsche, for whom it served to break the bounds of the treatise, to take a hammer to the form of philosophy, only to be bound up in the constraints of a disjunctive, discursive mode. But that is the least of its troubles, for its name binds us to a certain lineage – to, of all things, a theology.

2. Basket Case

Imagine Paul breaking the bounds. Shortly after breaking out of the Pharisaic mode (Pharisee meaning 'separated') and declaring himself a follower of Jesus, he finds he has to escape in a hurry from Damascus: 'They watched the gates day and night to kill him. Then the disciples took him by night, and let him down by the wall in a basket' (Acts 9: 24). You see what happens. There is no end to the constraints: you escape from the enclosure of a religious separation, only to find yourself circled about by enemies. You plan your escape only to find yourself enclosed in an even tighter space: to get over the wall, you have to get into a basket. The basket is both a metaphor and an aphorism: a transport and a confinement. Escape and return.

3. Pagan and Peasant

In pursuing the aphorism, we cannot avoid parables. It is Agamben, he who hates parables, who returns us to the parable of the Pharisee and the peasant in pursuit of the meaning of the aphorism. The Pharisees, he says, separated themselves both from the pagans and from the peasants who did not know the law.[1] This is not one parable but many, for it is this very separation that seems to underlie the parabolic sequence that includes the story of the prodigal son in Luke 15. The sequence begins with this separation; it is part of the framing narrative, and could, on a certain interpretation, even be said to be the *raison d'être* for these particular parables: 'And the Pharisees and scribes murmured, saying, This man receiveth sinners, and eateth with them' (Luke 15: 2). The complaint is that Jesus is not a Pharisee; he is not a separated one. He receives and joins in. The very next words of the chapter set up the parables as a response to this perception of the need for separation: 'And he spake this parable unto them, saying . . . ' In this light, the parables oppose separation; they are tales told in the interests of integration. Yet each parable is a separate nugget of narrative form, an aphoristic tale.

4. Parable and Apologue

Unsurprisingly, the separation of the Pharisee from the peasant who does not know the law, reminds Agamben of Kafka's parable 'Before the Law'. Agamben carefully does not call Kafka's story a parable; he finds another term, another genre – 'apologue' (meaning 'moral fable') – in order to separate the story from the class of parables; to make it a parable of parables.[2] Parables are too unruly; strangely, they are not sufficiently messianic.

5. 'Some fabulous yonder'

It is clear in the meta-parable 'On Parables', that Kafka knew just how difficult it could be to handle parables. This curious little piece stages a confrontation between those who think parables are liberating fictions capable of transforming our experience of the mundane, and those who see them as worthless mystifications that deflect attention from present, earthly problems by turning them into figures of 'some fabulous yonder'. The closing exchange between apologists for each position is both funny and troubling:

> One man said: 'Why do you resist? If you followed the parables, then you would become parables yourselves, and thus free of your daily cares.'
> Another said: 'I bet that is also a parable.'
> The first said: 'You have won.'

The second said: 'But unfortunately only in parable.'
The first said: 'No, in reality; in parable you have lost.'[3]

Who has won the argument? The answer depends entirely upon which
viewpoint you take. What I mean is this: the Anti-parable voice stands
outside of the Pro-parable voice's reasoning, separating itself from a logic
that seeks to enfold it. All it has to do to resist is to say that everything
brought against its argument is parable, and therefore worthless. This
cannot be disproved since a parable only works inasmuch as the tale it tells
is strictly within the limits of the everyday, and so nothing can be said to
be, *a priori*, outside of the ambit or purview of the parable. The category
effectively becomes meaningless because it does not separate itself from real
life. The parable becomes nothing more than an interpretation of, or a
perspective upon, the everyday. This, presumably, is why the Pro-parable
voice concedes that the Anti-parable voice has won. But as soon as this
victory is secured, the logic flips, because if everything sublunary can be
attributed to, or is captured by, parable, then that includes this exchange,
and the apparent victory is itself parabolic. Hence the assertion that in
parable the victor has lost. This, in turn, flips the logic again since it would
mean that loss becomes a parable of victory, so that rather than representing
everyday life, parable misrepresents it, turns it inside out. I suspect that this
flipping may continue indefinitely. You may disagree with my logic. You
win.

6. Unstable Persistence

Parable is never stable in its relation to the real. This is partly because stories
call to one another, echo one another, evoke one another, in a way that
excludes a direct connection with the real by means of a detour through
other stories; and it is partly because (as Kafka demonstrates), just when you
have grasped a parabolic relation, it slips your grasp and changes into something else. But the fact that the relationship is not stable does not mean that
it does not exist or that it is not worthwhile. The story of the prodigal son,
in which unstable relationships persist, makes that clear.

7. The Catholic

Paul, it seems, the figure of the death of parable, is also an aphorism.
Agamben pursues the problem posed by Paul's self-description as 'sepa-

rated', over against his universalism: his propagation of 'the "Catholic" vocation of the messianic community.'[4] Agamben is commenting on the first verse of the first chapter of Romans: 'Paul, a servant of Jesus Christ, called to be an apostle, separated unto the gospel of God'. Separated – *aphorismenos*. While he refers to himself as a separated one, Paul also seems to announce 'the messianic end of all separation between Jews and pagans.' So not only is he an aphorism, but he is also a parable, since a parable is a separate story that announces the end of separation. There is an issue, then, between the aphorism and the parable that Paul, parabolically, embodies.

8. God's Chopper

(a) Since to leave one place, group, situation, is to enter another, separation is never itself; it is always separated from itself by a kind of interior geography – more accurately, by a *law*, for Agamben sees the problem in terms of law. The argument goes something like this: the law divides us between those that have it, or know it, or have access to it, and those like the figure in Kafka's parable / apologue, who are before it without access to it. We are split between Pharisees and peasants, I suppose. But Paul proposes another division: the messianic aphorism that divides the very division effected by the law. For Agamben's Paul, the law is primarily a division, a line that separates Jew from non-Jew. But the messianic aphorism divides again, cutting into the division, re-drawing the lines, realigning the parts. Thus both the Jew and the non-Jew are divided, in Pauline parlance, between the 'spirit' and the 'flesh', implying that not all Jews are Jews, and not all non-Jews are non-Jews. There are Jews that are Jews according to the flesh, but not according to the spirit; and there are Jews that are Jews according to the sprit, but not according to the flesh. The same, *mutatis mutandis*, applies to non-Jews. This, as Agamben observes, 'leaves a remnant on either side which cannot be defined either as a Jew or a non-Jew.'[5] The remnant must remain a question for now. If the argument seems technical, dependent upon a rhetoric of subtle tmesis, we should remember that in the background is a *story* of multiple severance: the conversion narrative Paul tells of his own experience, according to which he was *separated* from his mother's womb (Galatians 1:5), from Pharisaism, and from his old self. By virtue of the messianic cutting that makes an aphorism of the convert, the life becomes a parable of the law.

(b) The remnant is an offcut – the by-product of the messianic. Paul's life is a parable of that too: 'we are made as the filth of the world, and are the offscouring of all things unto this day' (1 Cor. 4: 13). Why? Precisely because he was made an apostle: 'For I think that God hath set forth us the apostles last . . . ' (1 Cor. 4: 9). Being made an apostle is the unkindest cut of all; it is the thing for which one is separated, according to Romans 1:1, and therefore, the thing that makes one an offcut, an accidental, detached form. The aphorism makes of the apostle a parable of the remnant.

9. Cut to the Chase

With every cut a parable is born.

10. Analysis

Analysis produces stories.

11. The Remnant

The remnant is that which returns, that which comes home again after its exile. It is a figure that Paul takes over from the prophets, especially from Isaiah (10:20–22), but also from the minor prophets. The remnant has a messianic significance that can be seen in Micah 4: 7 where it is associated with ingathering, healing, comfort and restoration: 'And I will make her that halted a remnant, and her that was cast far off a strong nation: and the Lord shall reign over them in mount Zion from henceforth, even for ever.' Although traditionally the remnant has been understood (by Christian interpreters, anyway) as a portion, subset, or numerical remainder of Israel, Agamben construes it as a particular, messianic relation: it is neither part nor all; rather it is the result of the messianic aphorism that divides the divisions in such a way that neither whole nor part can be identified. And this remnant, Agamben thinks, Paul sees as a present reality.

Of course, this is part of the argument about universalism, and it raises the issue of what 'universal' can possibly mean in the context of the messianic, if, as Agamben's Paul claims, the already arrived messianic applies to, and is inextricably interwoven with, the curious figure of the remnant. The question is political, for Agamben. The logic of the remnant implies that there is no universality in the sense of absolute sameness or equality, but that in relation to the messianic 'every people will necessarily situate itself as a remnant, as not all.'[6] I do not need to say that the messianic comes to the political only by way of the parable. This is not simply because the politics of the left imagined its new state as the republic of heaven (to borrow a phrase from Philip Pullman), but also because, as we have seen, the remnant is that which was lost and is found, that which went astray and has come home again. It is precisely this narrative shape that allows the political to be mapped onto the messianic: without the return of the lost there is no remnant.

Skin Trunk
Literature and Resistance in *Father and Son*

There is in the nature or culture of the carceral, whether viewed from the perspective of the controlling system, or from that of the controlled subject, a tendency to call forth literary responses: the writing or reading of narratives of confinement, torture, survival, escape, or poetic resistance to the restricting of human potential. This is a fact that has implications not only for literature itself, but also for the oppressive systems that impose physical and psychological restraints upon individuals.

Literature seems to be demanded by incarceration not only because the writing that emerges from captivity serves to expose the abuses of the powerful – the captors, guards, inquisitors and torturers – by directly depicting their egregious behaviour, but also because both writing and reading provide forms of psychological release for the imprisoned consciousness. This much is obvious from the long history of the literatures of captivity, going back at least as far as Bunyan. But, there is another dimension to the relationship between literature and the control systems that impose their hatred of freedom on the dissident: literature is often constituted as the breach in the prison wall, the ungovernable operation within the mechanism, or the virus in the software of statehood. This may be because, characteristically, it draws attention to the unmasterable, the anomalous, to the aspects of human experience and potential that lie at the edges of what is assimilable within whatever passes for 'normal' patterns of thought and behaviour. But it is also because of the excess of meaning in the literary text: the content that can never be mastered, repeated or conceptualised within the critical response or reading. 'Our interest,' as Robert Browning put it so memorably, 'is on the dangerous edge of things,' and literature fashions, feeds and flaunts that interest.[1]

With this in mind, this chapter examines a text that stands on the edge of Victorianism, leaning in to modernism – appearing at a moment when the character and functions of literature were undergoing a radical reappraisal, and when the critical response to it was taking on new rigour and professionalism.[2] Edmund Gosse's *Father and Son* tells a story of imprisonment and escape at the heart of which is the relationship between a carceral religion, and imaginative literature as the flaw or stress point in the walls of its citadel. Taking its cue from Derrida's perception that no practice is ever totally faithful to its principle, it can be argued that Gosse's text reveals the gap between the principle and practice of carceral systems, allowing the reader to find in the imaginative response to literature a site of effective resistance.[3] As Gosse himself puts it: ' . . . in religious more than in any other matters, there is a perpetual contradiction between our thoughts and our deeds which is inevitable to our social order.'[4] That 'perpetual contradiction' is itself the formation of a kind of fiction that invites an imaginative response.

For Edmund Gosse, the love of literature and the love of his father were at odds with each other, and his discovery of literature is characterised in *Father and Son* as his means of escape, not from a cruel father whom he did not love, but from an over-anxious parent who tried to control his inner life. One aspect of that control was the banning of most imaginative literature, especially fiction, from the family home:

> No fiction of any kind, religious or secular, was admitted into the house. In this it was to my Mother, not to my Father, that the prohibition was due. She had a remarkable, I confess to me still somewhat unaccountable impression that to 'tell a story', that is, to compose fictitious narrative of any kind, was a sin. She carried this conviction to extreme lengths. (24)

When, eventually, young Gosse was allowed to read a novel, he says, 'It was like giving a glass of brandy neat to some one who had never been weaned from a milk diet' (160). This is his description of a significant early encounter with an adventure story:

> There were certain scenes and images in *Tom Cringle's Log* which made not merely a lasting impression upon my mind, but tinged my outlook upon life. The long adventures, fightings and escapes, sudden storms without, and mutinies within, drawn forth as they were, surely with great skill, upon the fiery blue of the boundless tropical ocean, produced on my inner mind a sort of glimmering hope, very vaguely felt at first, slowly developing, long stationary and faint, but always tending towards a belief that I should escape at last from the narrowness of the life we led at home, from this bondage to the Law and the Prophets . . . the reading of *Tom Cringle's Log* did more than anything else, in this critical eleventh year of my life, to give fortitude to my individuality, which was in great danger – as I now see – of succumbing to the pressure my Father brought to bear upon it from all sides. My soul was shut up, like Fatima, in a tower to which no external influences could come, and it might really have been starved to death, or have lost the power

of recovery and rebound, if my captor, by some freak not yet perfectly accounted for, had not gratuitously opened a little window in it and added a powerful telescope. The daring chapters of Michael Scott's picaresque romance of the tropics were that telescope and that window. (161–2)

Here literature has the function of opening up a vista of possibilities, giving form to discontent, and evoking an uneasy self-awareness that is at odds with the religious milieu characterised by a 'bondage to the Law and the Prophets.' As in the case of Helen Keller, the self in Gosse's story is forti-fied, paradoxically, by that which contravenes it, coming in from outside in the form of literature. The incarcerated subject is not itself; it becomes itself when the world impinges in a textual form. The escape that is the finding of the self, is also the return of that which the self excludes: the other, the exterior, language already founded and shaped by forces beyond the ego.

It is no coincidence that escapes and mutinies were amongst the great attractions of this first sustained encounter with fiction. I say first 'sustained' encounter, for there is an account of an earlier *brief* encounter with fiction in *Father and Son;* I am working my way towards it. But, for now, we can note that Gosse's description of the scene of reading is perme-ated by the sense of an enclosed self in search of the fulfilment denied to it to the extent that home becomes a prison, and the father a jailer. The boy will eventually run away in order to find the world opened up for him by reading, and the world of reading will become a matter of self-identifica-tion for him, not only in that it will distance him from his father, but also in that he will eventually say that it is the most important thing to him, and the love of it a badge of office:

> If at the end of seventy years of life I have the good fortune to hold any special position, it is solely due to the fact that all through my life I have cared for literature and for nothing else. . . . Literature is so great, so constant a comfort, and it never fails.[5]

By the end of his life, Gosse had become not only an avid reader, but also the author of nearly fifty books.

Moments of reading, of engagement with imaginative literature, bring to light a breach in the carceral, parental world – a breach that has been there from the beginning. It is the 'unaccountable freak' that leads the captor to build a window into the prison – the metaphorical window consti-tuted by the presence of literary texts, whether the stray novel, *Tom Cringle's Log*, or other accidental contraband pages such as those towards which we are moving. If this window is a metaphor or conceit, it is also a matter of

real-world conditions in Gosse's experience. For, tellingly, it is in the pages
of the Bible – the founding text of the very system of control that limits the
boy's freedom – that little Edmund first encounters the literary sublime:

> It was my Father's plan from the first to keep me entirely ignorant of the
> poetry of the High Church, which deeply offended his Calvinism; he
> thought that religious truth could be sucked in, like mother's milk, from
> hymns which were godly and sound, and yet correctly versified; and I was
> therefore carefully trained in this direction from an early date. But my spirit
> had rebelled against some of these hymns . . .
>
> This summer, as my eighth year advanced, we read the 'Epistle to the
> Hebrews' with very great deliberation, stopping every moment, that my
> Father might expound it, verse by verse. The extraordinary beauty of the
> language – for instance, the matchless cadences and images of the first
> chapter – made a certain impression upon my imagination, and were (I
> think) my earliest initiation into the magic of literature. (73–4)

Each of these chinks in the curtain walls of Gosse senior's religious citadel
is literary, and each is the product of his own design rather than of his son's
disobedience. However carefully constructed the edifice may appear to be,
the thought is contradicted by the deed, the practice belies the principle.
The seed of rebellion and the conditions for escape are both set by the system
itself, in its doubleness or inconsistency. For there is a sense in which Gosse's
father is two: he is both captor and secret fomenter of resistance, a bit like
Stevenson's Doctor Jekyll, who is both Mr Hyde's jailer and his liberator.

This doubleness is encoded, significantly, in the religious imagery of
Father and Son. To the young Edmund, his father appears to be omniscient
and all-seeing: 'My Mother always deferred to my Father, and in his absence
spoke of him to me as if he were all-wise. I confused him in some sense with
God' (33). But when Gosse senior's abortive intervention in the evolution
versus creation debate (*Omphalos,* 1857) is almost universally panned, a
counter-image emerges:

> My Father was not prepared for such a fate. He had been the spoiled darling
> of the public, the constant favourite of the press, and now, like the dark
> angels of old,
>
> > so huge a rout
> > Encumbered him with ruin. (88)

The implied comparison, here, is – as Peter Allen observes – 'not with "dark angels" generally but with Satan.'[6] So the father, in the son's imagination, is both divine jailer overseeing a panopticon home, and a satanic rebel against divine authority. It is also noticeable that the image of God is not pinned down to any literary source, while the image of Satan appears in the form of a quotation from *Paradise Lost*: it is the rebel, the dissident, the refusenik rather than the figure of control or authority who is given licence by the work of literature.

Given the father's duality, it is no surprise that the boy splits in two, not once, but twice. Self division and its concomitant – interior monologue (or maybe dialogue) – occur early in the boy's life, not as an effect of the father's combination of contradictory roles, but as a mode of resistance to the totalitarianism of the evangelical belief system operated in the home: 'There was a secret in this world and it belonged to me and to a somebody who lived in the same body with me. There were two of us, and we could talk with one another' (35). Later on the reader can sense that the consolation of a second self is not enough, that the conflicting aspects of the father enforce another division in young Edmund: 'My spirits were divided pathetically between the wish to stay on, a guarded child, and to proceed into the world, a budding man' (226).

The words of Gosse's friend, Robert Louis Stevenson, in *The Strange Case of Dr Jekyll and Mr Hyde* (1886), spring to mind once more: 'I hazard the guess that man will be ultimately known for a mere polity of multifarious, incongruous and independent denizens.'[7] Self-multiplication later became a facet of Gosse's social existence; the early splitting of the self continued so that Gosse became a protean figure. Ann Thwaite writes: 'He would tend, genuinely I think, such were his feelings of sympathy and friendship, to agree with the person he was with, the correspondent he was writing to. It was not hypocritical; he really did see that particular version of events, that particular side of the story.'[8] Peter Allen makes a similar point:

> Gosse's use of language was habitually influenced more by his sense of audience than his sense of truth. His upbringing had left him much in need of affection, and he strove constantly to impress, to charm. In his correspondence he characteristically used the language of agnosticism to agnostics but did not hesitate to use the language of orthodox faith when writing to a Christian.[9]

The victory of audience over truth is that of literature over religion, imagination over control systems. Furthermore, as Allen observes, this overthrow is traceable to the operation of the repressive system itself. Such a chameleon-like quality could be interpreted as either a virtue or a vice; it could be excused psychologically or celebrated as open-mindedness. Or it could be taken as proof of Stevenson's amoral dictum about the multiplicity of the self – an idea that was emerging in the late Victorian period with the rise of psychology in the work of William James, Freud and others. However it is understood, it is allied in Gosse's life and writings with the dynamics of resistance and escape, with the forming of a self that was sufficiently slippery to elude control strategies, that would put it beyond the reach of external authority. It is also an effect of what Gosse calls the 'perpetual contradiction' of a social order predicated upon religious 'truth'. That is to say, that the exposure of the contradiction at the heart of a closed system is the irruption of fiction within it – the revelation of its internal exposure to that which it excludes. I might be thinking of critical procedures and the ways in which practice escapes their control precisely inasmuch as the creative operates within the critical.

The first realisation of inner doubleness comes in the wake of an incident that convinced Edmund that his father was neither omniscient nor infallible. The revelation is couched in terms of a fall: 'My Father, as a deity, as a natural force of immense prestige, fell in my eyes to a human level' (35). The site of this fall from grace, this strange garden, is a motherless world that Gosse himself describes as 'our Eveless Eden' – a point that I will return to shortly (125). Here the father is God, Satan and Adam, so that Gosse's role-model is self-contradictory, but absolute. He is both the progenitor and the scourge of rebellion, as well as the fallible miscreant. It seems that such self-divergence means that the return of the prodigal is, in a sense, prophesied, encoded in the very origins of rebellion, since prodigality is predicated upon a connection which it wants to escape, but upon which it also depends to make escape seem desirable or even possible. When Gosse explicitly imagines himself as 'The Prodigal', in his poem of that title, the imagery he employs is that of a seemingly inevitable return to the garden: 'Open thy garden-gate to one benighted' ('The Prodigal,' l. 43).[10] He is returning to what he refers to as the 'garden-land' of the poem's addressee (l. 28).

But return is not to a pristine, unchanged situation. Again, Gosse's poem makes that clear. The poem begins by recalling childhood dreams or fantasies of fame and success: 'A little while, he saith, and men must know me; / A few feet more, and I must reach the light' (ll. 5–6). But experience shows that 'The breathless ages prove a boy's delusion' (l. 11) and success when it comes is 'partial' (l. 15). The failure of youthful dreams leads the speaker to reassess his life, and to discover that their demise leaves an emptiness into which conscience creeps: 'Back rush old thoughts, familiar thoughts and tender, / That slumber'd in the conscience, dumb and deep' (ll. 19–20). These tender thoughts recall the 'garden-land' belonging to the addressee, and the speaker pleads to be taken back in: 'Ah! take me home; my pride of pinion broken' (l. 33). But the terms of the return are not straightforward:

I bring thee back thine old love for token
That I am he for whom it toiled and prayed.

Undone the toil, and vain the intercession!
But ah! beneath thy fire for my success
There lurked a hungry sense of lost possession
And for my failure thou'lt not love me less. (ll. 35–40)

Clearly, the returning prodigal is not quite repentant since he insists that the addressee's toil and prayer have not availed. Gosse would not return to the religion of his parents. He does not ask forgiveness. So a tension is set up between the appeal for renewed acceptance and an insistence that his homecoming is not to be seen as a re-assimilation into the old order. That tension puts great pressure on the two lines that come between the self-assertion and the bid for acceptance, in the sense that they have to mediate between the two poles of the speaker's ambivalence. 'Thy fire for my success' seems to suggest that the addressee was complicit with the now-dead dreams. But the next line indicates that there was a deeper-lying motivation – an acknowledgement that the prodigal's success was the addressee's loss: to gain a successful and independent child, is also to lose one's role as parent. So the ambivalence of the speaker about his own orientation towards his own past and present, is projected onto the addressee, or is imagined as deriving from parental doubleness or self-contradiction. Once again the origin of prodigality and rebellion cannot be securely located in either the captor or the captive, the father or the son, God or the devil. As a prodigal one both follows and does not follow one's progenitor(s)

It can be seen from the depiction of Gosse senior that Gosse junior's rebellion, his need to escape, is, in certain respects, a repetition of certain tendencies observable in his father. This often seems to be missed by critical accounts of his life and work. James D. Woolf, for example, writes:

Gosse's master faculty may be stated in one word, pleasure – which includes delight, joy, and delectation; for the idea of pleasure is the moving force behind his indefatigable studies and compositions . . . Pleasure as the essential faculty in Gosse's personality is readily traceable to the environment of his Puritan childhood. Severe restrictions on his behaviour, dismalness,

impatience, and anger were conditions that he desired to escape. And his
great delight in imaginative literature, a reaction against his youthful
Puritan environment, was the chief means of escape from such fetterings of
his personality.[11]

Seeing Gosse's aestheticism as a reaction against a Puritan upbringing is a
little too neat. It will not do, at least not without qualification, since, as has
been shown, the dynamics of domestic rebellion are neither unidirectional
nor simple in their origins and effects.

Gosse does not react against his upbringing without in certain ways
repeating it. Gosse senior was himself a dissenter from the religion of his
parents, who, in order to 'develop his own peculiar theology,' fled from
home at an early age to travel to Newfoundland, Canada, and later
Jamaica.[12] He, like his son, was a prodigious writer who produced nearly
fifty books. Edmund repeated in a different key not only his father's dissent,
travel and prodigious output, but also called his own son Philip after his
father, and took him on just the kind of beachcombing trips that were so
much a part of his own upbringing. He wrote to Hamo Thorneycroft in
1887: 'We have had such excitements as collecting cockles, catching prawns
in pools, bathing on the sands and climbing over the strange crimson
promontories; and Philip has been my companion in longer excursions
along the coast.'[13] *Father and Son* is replete with accounts of such jaunts with
that other Philip – Edmund's father. The lengths that Gosse senior went to
in order to keep his son from theological error can surely be seen as an effect
of his own rejection of the system that once enclosed him. Today's radical
is tomorrow's die-hard. Today's revolutionary is tomorrow's totalitarian.
Gosse thus illustrates that anacolouthon, following and not following, is
more than a rhetorical trope: it is enacted in the life of a writer. In Gosse's
case, the junction between the critical and the creative is also the moment
of continuity in discontinuity, of both following and not following his
father.

Since Gosse's need to escape is both a repetition and an innovation, it
can be characterised as both an inherited mindset and a material environment. He thus depicts his incarceration as both physical and psychological.
He describes the houses and gardens of his youth as a series of boundaries,
beyond which he was allowed to take limited and supervised excursions
under his father's licence:

That I might not be kept indoors all day and every day, a man . . . connected with the meeting-house, was paid a trifle to take me out for a walk
each morning . . . On one occasion, poor dreary man, he met a friend and

stopped to chat with him. I considered this act to have dissolved the bond; I skipped lightly away from his side, examined several shop windows which I had been forbidden to look into, made several darts down courts and up passages, and finally, after a delightful morning, returned home, having known my directions perfectly. My official conductor, in a shocking condition of fear, was crouching by the area-rails looking up and down the street. He darted upon me, in a great rage, to know 'what I meant by it?' I drew myself up as tall as I could, hissed 'Blind leader of the blind!' at him, and, with this inappropriate but very effective Parthian shot, slipped by him into the house. (56)

There is always a servant in the story of the prodigal. You will recall that in the parable, the servants act as psychological boundary figures for the destitute runaway: they serve to give value to the prodigal in his own estimation: he regains himself at their expense. If we read in the interests of the servant, then the boy's assertion of his self-will becomes a moment of class conflict: the hired help suffers for the insouciance of the self-absorbed masters. The process of individuation that we are meant to read, leaves the subordinate unnamed, and makes of him a figure, not quite of ridicule, but of instructive contrast with the burgeoning subjectivity of the author; he is effectively objectified. Here escape becomes not just return, but also itself a form of control and incarceration.

If this incident indicates something of Gosse's prodigal tendency – his desire to slip the leash and follow his own path, to encounter the forbidden (indifferent to the cost) – the fact that it is embedded within a passage about the premature loss of his mother suggests that something of what made him a prodigal lies in that bereavement. He records that in her dying days his mother 'tenderly and closely urged [his] Father, who, however, needed no urging, to watch with unceasing care over [his] spiritual welfare' (57). Much of the book is taken up with precisely this watchfulness, its intensity, its oppressiveness, and its tendency to have an effect more-or-less the opposite of its intention. The narrative strategy at this point seems designed to invest the mother's love, force of character, concern and piety in the father, so that, after her death, he embodies the system of control even more absolutely than the familiar Victorian paterfamilias.

But the father takes on more than just the mother's stringent proscriptions. Gosse depicts a relationship with his father that is tender, loving and intimate, in a way which few Victorian father–son stories match. Their Eden may be 'Eveless', but the father does have maternal qualities. The relationship between Gosse the father and Gosse the son can be sharply contrasted, for instance, with Samuel Butler's *The Way of All Flesh*, with its depiction of febrile dislike blossoming into hatred. The narrative thus encourages us to see young Edmund's rebellion as something other than a clash of temperaments, despite the book's somewhat misleading subtitle: it is about an individual striving for self-realisation. The closing lines make this clear: 'the young man's conscience threw off once for all the yoke of his "dedication," and, as respectfully as he could, without parade or remonstrance, he took a human being's privilege to fashion his inner life for himself' (250). By fashioning his inner life for himself, Gosse means something like this: the self is fashioned by literature.

As we have seen, it is at the very point where the narrative emphasises the common purpose and the conjoined energies of mother and father, that the son is seen momentarily escaping the domestic order in a proleptic moment of resistance, as though to emphasise that the rebellion to come will not be a straightforwardly Oedipal father killing: it is not so much a matter of escaping his father as an individual, as it is of evading the system he represents: Victorianism, evangelical Christianity, domesticity, close-mindedness etc. But not, it would seem, the political / economic system that feeds on the objectifying of the servant.

The context of domestic rebellion in which *Father and Son* might be understood was explored by Lee Krenis in 1978. His article is a useful reference point here as it offers compelling evidence that prodigality had a strong link with literary endeavour in the period. Discussing autobiographical texts by Charles Darwin, John Ruskin, J. A. Froude, Samuel Butler, J. S. Mill, and Herbert Spencer alongside *Father and Son,* he argues that the father-hating (or rebellion against patriarchs) evident in these narratives was a reaction to changing patterns that were breaking down traditional social ties in society at large, leading the middle class to become 'more isolated and emotionally intense.'[14]

> In contrast to a world where authority had come to be less simply defined, familial authority took on its own rigorous clarity. The point is not merely that fathers wielded power within the family as a matter of course. That had always been the case. What was new, in the more self-sufficient privacy of many families, was the potent consolidation of the father's authority as patriarch, teacher, and clergyman in presiding over his own small shelter from doubt and division.[15]

This is dramatically true in *Father and Son.* The sense of the home as an island, cut off from the affairs of the sublunary world is intensified by the religious zeal of Gosse senior, and by the absence of a mother for much of the narrative. The father encloses his home to keep out the sullied and

sullying world, making Edmund feel like a prisoner: 'I saw myself imprisoned for ever in the religious system which had caught me . . . I did not
struggle against it, because I believed that it was inevitable, and that there
was no other way of making peace with the terrible and ever-watchful "God
who is a jealous God" ' (157). Gosse senior's all-encompassing concern for
his son stems from that religious system, and from the fear that the boy will
fall from grace. As Krenis says: 'Behind the stress on discipline and close
surveillance lay the conviction that children were by nature sinful and easily
corrupted.'[16]

And where did the seeds of rebellion against this domestic enclosure and
control lie? In literature, of course:

> As a child Spencer, 'extremely prone to castle-building,' was addicted to
> Gothic horror novels . . . Gosse was able to fortify his individuality by
> reading and re-reading an ordinary adventure story that accidentally fell into
> his grasp. For Mill and Hale White, Wordsworth's poetry was a liberating
> influence . . . For the fictional Mark Rutherford, reading the *Lyrical Ballads*
> catalyzed a more direct rebellion against religious authority by enabling him
> to substitute an abstract, pantheistic 'God of the hills' for the patriarchal
> 'God of the Church.'[17]

In each case such a literature-based rebellion is understandable as stemming
from literature's ability to open gaps in the walls, to let in a light that this
particular form of Victorian religious patriarchy wanted to extinguish. This
was clearly so in Gosse's case, although the conduit of the prohibition in
this instance was, as we have seen, his mother. Interesting then that he
should think of his mother as misdirected: had she understood her own
talents and propensities, she should have been a literary figure:

> Was my Mother intended by nature to be a novelist? I have often thought
> so, and her talents and vigour of purpose, directed along the line which was
> ready to form, 'the chief pleasure of her life,' could hardly have failed to
> conduct her to great success. She was a little younger than Bulwer Lytton, a
> little older than Mrs Gaskell – but these are vain speculations. (26)

We have seen that the mother's absence intensifies the father's scrutiny and
control. Her absence from most of the boy's life is a factor in his incarceration, and this is of a piece with her signal failure to become a novelist, with
her rejection of the literature of imagination – her belief that 'to tell a story,
that is, to compose fictitious narrative of any kind, was a sin . . . ' So, in her
absence, literature – the embodiment of a lost mother – becomes a kindly

stepmother – a counter-influence to the imprisoning, patriarchal, religious domesticity of the father's house. The misplaced mother, the lost novelist, shows the errancy of the system, and she provides Gosse with an imaginary or fictional lineage that connects him to literary traditions, to Lytton and to Gaskell.

The sense of misdirection in his mother's life, and the similar failure that he attributes to his father – a good man misled by Puritanism – is also part of the pattern Gosse falls into, or imposes upon his own life. He was an inveterate literary misleader, famously inaccurate in just about all he did. Tennyson once said of him: 'I fear Mr G. is a most inaccurate man. He made three statements in his notice of me in the *St James Gazette,* all more or less false'.[18] Henry James wrote that Gosse had 'a genius for inaccuracy'.[19] More recently, Harold Orel has written of our 'suspicion that Gosse is not a completely reliable witness to what he knows or what he has read,' and of the latter's work as plagued by 'lacunae in needed information.'[20] Gosse's biographer, Ann Thwaite, convicts him of trafficking in unreliable dates, errors of fact, prevarication over his own religious beliefs, inaccuracy in translation, and lack of conscientiousness in the production of biographies. Each of these failings is recurrent. Not only so, but he was implicated (if only by default) in the forgeries of rare first editions by the infamous T. J. Wise.

Most notoriously, it was John Churton Collins who attacked what we might call Gosse's prodigal tendencies. In the *Quarterly Review* for October 1886, Collins accused Gosse of literary charlatanism, of being a mere journalist who passed himself off as a scholar. He went on to show that Gosse's latest book, *From Shakespeare to Pope,* claimed familiarity with texts its author had not read, that it contained inaccuracies with respect to dates, loose and flowery writing, spurious claims to various kinds of discoveries, and a pervasive ignorance when it came to the facts of literary history. If this was the most damning review Gosse received in his career, it was by no means the only one that took him to task for a want of scholarly rigour.

The Collins affair, at least as it is framed by Thwaite, suggests that Gosse may be seen as a crucial figure in the history and development of English literary criticism precisely because of his failures. Collins was peeved by Gosse's success not only because he envied his public acclaim and his appointment as Clark Lecturer at Trinity College, Cambridge in 1884, but also because he saw that appointment as indicative of the parlous state of literary studies in late Victorian Britain. 'Collins,' according to Orel, 'was the technical man, the professional scholar, who preferred accuracy to graciousness of style, and solid research to impressionistic maundering on literary topics.'[21] Collins might appear then to be in the vanguard of the professional study of English literature: a forebear to the academic critic, while Gosse represents that bad old dilettante tradition of *belle lettres.* Yet, we should not be too hasty to consign Gosse to the prehistory of the discipline. He was, after all, an innovator in a number of ways. He can (arguably) be credited with having introduced Ibsen and Gide to the English-speaking world, to have been the first English critic to have recognised the significance of Mallarme and the French symbolists, to have recovered the reputation of John Donne and to have produced, in *Father and Son,* a work of literature that bridged the gap between the Victorian novel and its modernist offspring. Not a bad list for somebody written off by the modernists as an inheritor of 'only the cant and fustiness' of the Victorian era, 'with a taste for kowtowing' (Ezra Pound),[22] and as a 'cold, cautious and clammy . . . writhing fat worm, red, shiny – disgusting' (Virginia Woolf).[23] He was everything the modernists thought they were against. There can be little more influential a position than that.

These achievements are taken a little more seriously at the start of the twenty-first century than they were in the early years of the twentieth, thanks largely to the work of critics such as Ann Thwaite and James D. Woolf. Yet in 1977 Frederic R. Ross summed up Gosse as 'literary critic, minor poet, biographer, salon keeper, sycophantic gadabout *par excellence,'*[24] and even as recently as 1984 he was dismissed by Harold Orel as 'a snob of the worst kind . . . [who] never knew enough to be accounted a professional.'[25] Over the years, attacks on Gosse have tended towards this kind of ad hominem tirade inspired, I suspect, by the attitudes of the Bloomsbury set who knew him personally and for whom he became the embodiment of defunct Victorianism. Modernism necessarily perceives itself as breaking with Victorianism, represented in its own time by Gosse. Yet, since he was an innovator, both in his criticism and in the literary form of *Father and Son* (which Peter Allen argues, with some justification, to be an important precursor to Joyce's *Portrait of the Artist*), there is a sense in which Modernism thrives on its Victorian inheritance.[26] Gosse is the father whose religion they must escape, one who built into his textual edifice the breaches that his detractors, the rebels against his critical house, would exploit. And so it goes. He embodies anacolouthon, in that he is a self-styled prodigal, and in that he represents the turning point between belles lettres and academic criticism, as well as that between Victorianism and Modernism. He is a figure of the following that does not follow.

I have no interest in taking sides here. I feel myself strongly disinclined to lionise a man who loved the aristocracy, served as librarian to the House of Lords, and ended his days as a Peer of the Realm. But I have to confess that he does interest me, mainly because of the double binary that seems to cling to him, making him a divisive figure: critic versus creative writer, impressionistic versus scholarly criticism. The two pairs are not wholly distinct since it often seems to be the case that Gosse's lack of scholarly assiduousness, his well-documented lack of rigour, is precisely what makes his literary critical work of enduring significance, pushing it – in one direction – towards the creative node, and opening – in the other, a breach that professional critics could exploit.

His greatest achievement – the uncategorisable *Father and Son,* is a product of this tension, being a highly self-conscious literary composition that masquerades as an historically factual account. The Preface claims that 'at one point only has there been any tampering with precise fact' (5), but a number of commentators have pointed to the discrepancies between the 'precise facts' in *Father and Son* and those recorded in his earlier biography of his father, as well as contradictions between *Father and Son* and other documentary sources. Thwaite, in introducing Gosse to her readers, highlights his characteristic tendency to misremember, to get things wrong and to fictionalise his own life:

> Gosse described himself as a 'tainted source' when someone was compiling a bibliography of his work. How much more so can this be said with regard to his own biography. Not only did his memory betray him. He also changed things deliberately very often to make a better story.[27]

Ross offers a number of examples of Gosse's tendency to mislead, especially when it came to representations of his father:

> the entire *Omphalos* incident as depicted in *Father and Son* is of doubtful veracity;

> did [the] almost total public rejection of *Omphalos* have the effect on Gosse [senior] that Edmund claims? Specifically, did it render him the taciturn, morbid recluse indicated in *Father and Son?* Probably not. At least this characterization stands in utter opposition to the description Edmund gives in the *Life*;

> Practiced in the extreme, as in the *Omphalos* incident, his tactics transform fact into something that approaches pure fiction.[28]

In the essay already cited, Peter Allen does an excellent job of highlighting not only such material inaccuracies, but also the artful, novelistic elements in the composition of *Father and Son*: its careful contrasts between the individual and the social/domestic environment, the establishing of a complicity with the reader that encourages us to see ourselves as more enlightened than the religious enthusiasts he describes, the parallels with Dickens' Pip in *Great Expectations*, and so on. As early as 1937 Edgar Johnson observed that the details laid out in *Father and Son* were selected on novelistic principles and were adopted self-consciously to produce a dramatic and compelling story.[29] In fact, something of the artifice such critics have diagnosed is obvious from the Preface. In the first place, it has a critical dimension that seeks to place the book carefully in its literary context:

> The author has observed that those who have written about the facts of their own childhood have usually delayed to note them down until age has dimmed their recollections. Perhaps an even more common fault in such autobiographies is that they are sentimental, and are falsified by self-admiration and self-pity. (5)

The reader is invited here to compare Gosse's narrative with other similar works, and to admit its superiority. At this point the 'self-admiration' which he calls a 'fault' that 'falsifies' other autobiographies, appears to be characteristic of this one. Another distinguishing factor that establishes the ascendancy of *Father and Son* over comparable volumes is its truth to life, perceived now not as factual accuracy, but as the continuation of distinctly literary traditions:

> It is not usual, perhaps, that the narrative of a spiritual struggle should mingle merriment and humour with a discussion of the most solemn subjects. It has, however, been inevitable that they should be so mingled in this narrative. It is true that most funny books try to be funny throughout, while theology is scandalised if it awakens a single smile. But life is not constituted thus, and this book is nothing if it not a genuine slice of life. There was an extraordinary mixture of comedy and tragedy in the situation which is here described, and those who are affected by the pathos of it will not need to have it explained to them that the comedy was superficial and the tragedy essential. (6)

Tragedy and comedy. As Peter Allen has observed, the father becomes a kind of tragic hero – a good, genteel man with a tragic flaw (his religious fervour).

Perhaps we can say that it is the detour through literary form, through the kind of misdirection that points to fact while weaving a fiction, the following of an untrue path, the prodigal moment, that makes Gosse worth reading. It is certainly the case that at the height of his powers Gosse was valued for something other than accuracy. His life of Gray elicited this response from Robert Louis Stevenson: 'I have read your *Gray* with care. A more difficult subject I can scarce fancy: it is crushing; yet I think you have managed to shadow forth a man, and a good man too; and honestly, I doubt if I could have done the same.'[30] This despite the fact that the biography contained material errors and had been written in just four months when he was working every day at the Board of Trade. What seemed to matter to most of his literary readers at the time was the impressionistic and evocative way in which he had created a vivid image of his subject, rather than that he had failed to do his research either exhaustively or even competently. 'None but a poet could have written of a poet with such sympathy,' was how Thomas Woolner put it.[31] Gosse was a stylist. Even his conversation is reputed to have had a beguiling effect, especially when he was embroidering the facts in order to turn real life into the form of a memorable story – a tendency his biographers repeatedly note.

The misdirection that Gosse perceived to have taken his mother away from fiction, then, took Gosse himself away from the mothering father and her / his proscription of fiction, and it took him towards what we are led to think of as a fiction of motherhood, or the motherhood of fiction. Little wonder, then, that the young Edmund encountered his first imaginative text inside an enclosed, womb-like space that, in Gosse's description, has connotations of the human body and of birthing:

> The garret was a fairy place. It was a lean-to, lighted from the roof. It was wholly unfurnished, except for two objects, an ancient hat-box and still more ancient skin-trunk . . . The skin-trunk was absolutely empty, but the inside of the lid of it was lined with sheets of what I now know to have been a sensational novel. It was, of course, a fragment, but I read it, kneeling on the bare floor, with indescribable rapture. It will be recollected that the idea of fiction, of a deliberately invented story, had been kept from me with entire success. (36)

Either side of this vignette lie memories of the lost mother that entwine with the partial narrative: 'I fancied that my mother, who was out so much, might be threatened by dangers of the same sort [as those faced by the "lady of title" in the fragment]; and the fact that the narrative came abruptly to an end, in the middle of one of its most thrilling sentences, wound me up almost to a disorder of wonder and romance' (36–7). The mother herself, like the truncated narrative, came abruptly to an end. And that romantic disorder is, of course, a figure of her loss. But it is also the undoing of the domestic system, or, at least, its transformation into fiction. The mother becomes a fiction; fiction becomes a mother; this is some kind of resistance, some kind of freedom: the birth of the lover of literature, the origin of his self-definition.

But we should not forget the servant whom we left crouching in fear by the railings. He may *still* be behind bars.

'**I**'

The first person is rare in parables. As it is in critical discourse. All the more reason to speak of it now, since escape is on the agenda. Escape *is* the agenda.

I keep thinking of Nietzsche, not only because his style involved disrupting philosophy with poetry, refusing the distinction between the critical and creative, but also because I am both charmed and made despondent by his notion that 'I' is a fiction, or that I am a stranger to myself. Poor old Descartes in his stove, warming his unreconstructed arse, was deluded, I know, and I am both exhilarated and desperate in this knowledge. The charm of it is that the diffuse, polyvalent, polyumbilicate, protean self is unleashed, free of the fixity that once made it a dull, entrammelled soul, encased in its ossified identity. I no longer *have* to be anything. But, on the down side, there is also something I *cannot* be: the one thing I want to be more than anything else: myself. I am not myself. I cannot be myself, since I am a discursive, decentred, interpellated subject. You don't have to tell me. But I don't want to be a fiction; I don't want to be a culturally conditioned tissue of effects woven from genes, language and ideology, a bio-discursive phenomenon devoid of ess**ce. I want to be a self-generating, free-standing s**l.

They call it the 'bourgeois humanist individual', this passé, unregenerate phantom that imagines itself a world-creating, self-determining force of nature, gestating a self-engendered ego in the hothouse of bad faith. And they are probably right. But I can't help it – the idea, sense, consciousness, or image, is too deeply rooted. Like the prodigal son, I have been at work, engaged in unfulfilling labour – not in pigsties, but in offices, warehouses, supermarkets – and have at such moments 'come to myself': heard the inner voice that called me back to a self beyond the function ascribed by alienating work – a self fashioned by the lyrics of Bob Dylan, Joni Mitchell, Leonard Cohen, Jackson Browne. And at such moments I have wanted to be something like I imagine Stephen Dedalus to be, as he encounters for the millionth time the reality of experience and desires to forge in the smithy of his soul the uncreated conscience of his race. Race? Maybe not. I am happy to acknowledge that race is a fiction, but a Welshness without borders matters to me; that is part of what I'd like to forge. To forge myself: artifice and counterfeit. This is sinful, I know. Cultural materialism, psychoanalysis, poststructuralism, feminism, and possibly even postcolonial theory are ranged against me. Against the fictional me, that is. Subjectivity is nothing personal.

What I saw (or what I imagined there was an I to see) when I first discovered Dedalus, was the ess**ce of what literature was to me in the beginning: self-discovery, self-expression. I suppose it is ironic that I know about all the things ranged against the self just because I read literature and books about literature, and did so in the first place because of a sense that people like me seemed to have written the books. You will know, perhaps, what I mean by 'people like me'. Some will know: 'white, male, European'; some will know: 'bourgeois man'; some will know: 'Eurocentric Anglophone'; some will know 'the implied author'; some will know: 'the truth effect of an imitative discursive practice'. I am a broken doll, my parts scattered across the library carpet. But I would like 'me' to mean something like the one who sits at home avidly watching old sitcoms on DVD, who sends out poems to magazines, who smokes four rollies a day, who goes to watch Cardiff City playing at Ninian Park, who listens to Radio Four at every opportunity, who plays the guitar and sings Bob Dylan songs in the bedroom; not the me who is writing this, obviously. (Was it Bloom who said 'There are no texts; there are only ourselves'?)

This was how it was when I first read *A Portrait of the Artist* at the age of nineteen. I read it because my elder brother told me I'd like it, and I happened to see a copy of the old Penguin Modern Classics edition in a box on a market stall for just 10p. Someone had told my brother the same thing, I suppose, and he liked it. And I liked it. I liked it because it was about a self in its inwardness, and Joyce had found words that brought into visibility the regions of interiority that I thought I knew by experience. I imagined in my innocence, or in my complicity, that I recognised the self. I underlined passages that seemed to speak my own feelings, and often went back to them. Someone like me still does.

Twenty years passed. At a conference in Bordeaux I bought a copy of *Ulysses*. By now, a little too late in life to be successful, I had become an academic. It was the academic who read *Ulysses*, but not for teaching or research purposes. Not for pleasure either, as it turned out. On many occasions since then I have discussed *Ulysses* with colleagues. The conversations tend to begin something like this:

Kevin:	I hate bloody *Ulysses*.
Real Scholar:	Really? I think it's superb.
Kevin:	It's very . . . clever. I can see that it's very clever, but it doesn't do anything for me. It doesn't move me, or challenge me, or shock me, or thrill me. It just

	seems to play intellectual games with language. I just end up thinking: so what?
Real Scholar:	That's what I like. Those games are fascinating.
Kevin:	*{Wistfully}.* Mm.

The 'Mm' encodes a feeling that blends alienation, disappointment and nervousness. It voices a fear that I am simply too stupid to understand Joyce, and a shamefaced, guilty, longing for the old 'I', for the self-portrait a young man found in the earlier book: the self lost in language-games, riddles, puns, allusions, irreducible textuality.

I wonder if you are now despising me, or (worse) if you are thinking that I am implying a kind of superiority, a greater authenticity of soul (forgive the obscenity) by ironically labelling my fictional or allegorical interlocutor 'Real Scholar', and voicing an almost Lawrentian sensitivity as a pointed contrast to the hollow cleverness of Joyceans. Maybe. But some of my best friends and favourite colleagues have been Joyceans, and I cannot bear Lawrence. So that's not quite it. What I seem to be circling around, teasing you (and myself) with, is the sense I have that I am not, never have been, never will be, a scholar, and that this has to do with a relationship with the academy that is neither hot nor cold, but, what the author of the book of Revelation would call 'Laodicean'. Again, it has to do with my relationship with literature: one that belongs to a kind of post-romantic, belletrist, hippy delight in myself and my relationship with language. This, I think, is why I am always on the run.

I have learned the games, you understand. I have served my apprenticeship in theory, textual analysis, rhetoric, continental philosophy and so on. I quite like some of it. Some of it actually changed my life. But there I go again; I can't stay away from the life-relation, the 'self-understanding' as hermeneuts once called it.

I am a prodigal.
You know I'll be back.

The Estate

I came across it by accident on entering the word 'prodigal' into the computer system of my university library, more in hope than expectation. It is a novel called *A Prodigal Child*, and it was written by David Storey.[1] As I begin to write I have not read it.

Before I read, I wonder how I should read it. How can I make it work for me? It has to work. I cannot invest the time in reading something that will not succumb to my design, or that cannot be shaped to my purpose without undue violence. It is not enough just to read; there is no guarantee that reading will translate to writing. Something alchemical has to happen that transmutes the base text into critical gold. This is the prodigal nature of the critic: we begin with an idea of what might be out there waiting for us, and we risk our time and energies on venturing into the unknown territory of the new text. And then we take it home, dragging the recalcitrant story by the scruff of the text into conformity with our preset programmes – producing our shaped and crafted reading.

A reading is not reading. Reading is just letting the text happen to you, while ideology, memory, imagination and genes make the words dance. *A reading* is the choreographic text: the construction of a score or diagram, an anatomising and a selection, a focusing and an excision.

I begin to read *A Prodigal Child*, without a score, but with a shaping expectation. Somewhere between reading and *a reading*, I suppose, examining, or at least allowing to appear, the process by which the one morphs into the other.

. . .

I read what seems to be a prologue. It is a short, poetic history of a place transformed from feudal estate into housing estate. There must be something about the story that will play on these two related, but very different, meanings of 'estate'. And maybe a third meaning is implied: that which is left at death: that which will be inherited by the survivors. Good. Inheritance is good; it suits my purposes. I am optimistic now.

The first chapter tells of a couple – the Morleys – with a young child – Alan – moving into a house on the new estate. Mr Morley returns a borrowed cart, gets drunk and is very late home. There is tension between the husband and wife. I am reminded of Hardy in the descriptions of movement between rural and urban, the picture of the man on the cart, the foolish drunkenness that I feel might cost Mr Morley and his wife dear. Already the academy calls to me through the text; I hear echoes of Hardy and I think about influence, tradition, the realist novel, and how this work might fit into the ready-made framework of critical categories.

The boy, who is a young child, will, perhaps, be our prodigal. He will, I suspect, run away from a father who loves him, but who drinks too much. Here, another frame of reference competes with the academic: the pattern of religious narrative evoked by the title. This is not altogether distinct from the literary framework of the English novel since the latter has always drawn on biblical sources – from Fielding's *Joseph Andrews* to Winterson's *The Passion*. Yet they seem at odds somehow. Maybe just because the Bible has gone out of fashion and the stories it tells are drifting into desuetude.

Money too is an issue for the Morleys. This couple cannot really afford their new home, so maybe our prodigal will want to escape poverty. He will probably become a writer of plays. Or an actor.

Chapter two gives Mrs Morley's prehistory as an unwanted and neglected last child among eight, the courtship of the Morleys, and another drinking episode. The estate, I think, is a council estate, since the Morleys are said to have been 'allocated' the house (23). This is appealing to me as I live on a council estate, though many of us who reside here have now bought our houses. The 'estate' in Storey's novel is slowly changing its meaning.

Apart from the drinking, I have noticed two features in the first two chapters which may be the beginning of patterns. During both of the drinking episodes, Morley notices that he is without his watch (12 & 30). Again I recall Hardy and the references to watches and telling the time by natural means in *Far From the Madding Crowd*.[2] It is said of Morley that 'he had no facility for telling the time at night, and he had taken his watch off earlier that evening' (30). He is caught, perhaps, between times: he has been a soldier and is now a farmhand; he travelled the world and must now settle down; he lives on an estate which has moved from feudal to municipal ownership, but works on a farm owned by another man; he is sensitive to nature and his own feelings, but seemingly insensitive towards his wife.

The other repeated feature, which may become a pattern, is the sense of surveillance on the estate, or, at least the fear that others might be watching, and the desire to keep up appearances. Chapter one ends:

She was standing there as if nothing had happened . . . she had come down to indicate that nothing was amiss . . .

'If you've cooked it, love,' he continued, in a voice loud enough to be heard outside, 'it'll be good enough for me'. (19)

In Chapter two there is a similar kind of gesture – a worry about who might be watching or listening: 'Since the houses opposite were in darkness, and a light was showing only in Patterson's scullery window, he called again, "Sarah!" between cupped hands' (28). Such repetitions, echoes, or motifs are crucial to the construction of *a reading*. There must be pattern. This is a shared feature of narrative and argument – neither can function in the absence of repetition.

. . .

Although in the time of reading it is probable that almost no time has passed since you read the last sentence, in the time of writing some weeks have gone by. For, I have to confess that it has been the best part of two months since I have read anything of the novel under discussion. Pressure of work. In the meantime, I have discovered John Lyly's Euphues – a Renaissance (should that be 'early-modern'?) prodigal. I shall probably not write about him here. The book is hard to like, not only because of its euphuism, but also because its hero turns into a sententious bore. That is the danger of being a prodigal, of course, you might return to the fold a pious oaf who has learned their lesson too well.

It is difficult now to pick up the dropped threads of the narrative, or to recover the sense of patterning that was just beginning to emerge. But at least this gives me a chance to suggest one more sense in which the critical process is prodigal: reading, for the busy critic with no research leave, is usually a matter of departure and return, of broken or interrupted relationships with texts, ideas, thought-processes. The polished reading, like a welcome-home party, carefully covers the discontinuities.

. . .

Chapter three introduces new next-door neighbours: Mr and Mrs Foster and their little daughter Alison. The Fosters seem to be the ideal family: happy, industrious, conventional, a little better paid than their neighbours. The fact that Mr Foster is a policeman introduces a sense of law, of control, of social norms and expectations, that contrast neatly (too neatly, perhaps) with the Morleys' slightly below-par social performance. Morley's drinking continues, money problems worsen, and, eventually Mrs Morley takes little Alan and flees back to her mother. Morley twice goes to the house in town to bring them home. On both occasions I feared that violence might erupt, but aside from the mother-in-law pummelling Morley's back, and one feeble attempt by the father to grab the little boy from his wife's arms, it does not materialise. My expectations were rather more violent than Mr Morley. Eventually, mother and child return following the intervention of the wife of Morley's employer – Mrs Spencer.

Around the Morleys, the new estate is coming to life, and a community is burgeoning. I like this picture of an optimistic moment – the sense of a kind of pioneering settlement of the working classes on the estate of the dead feudal landowners. I am thinking of the servants whose stories I have (occasionally) been tracing. Here they are – inheriting the estate, gathering under the banner of the civic corporation. I am trying not to think of what is to come – of the way in which we dwellers in council houses will buy into the 'property-owning democracy', or 'popular capitalism', of the Thatcher years, that will turn such communities into atomised, hermetic little fractions of 'estate'. When the novel was published in 1982 that process was just beginning.

At the end of the chapter, Morley seems contrite – beaten by necessities perhaps.

Another child arrives in the fourth chapter – another boy – called Bryan. But much of the chapter is taken up with Morley's habit of stealing small quantities of food from the farm on which he works, and with his worsening relationship with his wife. He feels trapped by the marriage because Sarah seems to him determined to make his life as narrow as possible. He fails to see that this narrowness is a necessary effect of bringing up a family on insufficient wages. I hear a faint echo of Rosamund Vincy/Lydgate in *Middlemarch*, as she fails to grasp the financial necessities that drive her husband to economise. I cannot escape these echoes. The novel is not itself for me; appropriately or not, other texts interfere.

The Morleys are growing to hate each other now. Both parents seem to be beginning to invest their hopes in their sons, and each of them is gradually resigning from the task of self-fulfilment. When Morley ponders the morality of his illicit acquisition of necessary food, reasoning that he is taking no more than his due as an underpaid employee, he dismisses the socialist strategy of nationalisation as likely to remove his incentive to work hard and to take pride in his work. He both admires and resents the farmer and reasons that the conflict of interests is necessary to them both: 'without that conflict there was nothing' (55). But the crucial point, I think, is that rather than working through the implications of this view, he puts his faith in the next generation: 'at some point in the future, his son, or his sons, might be able to resolve his problem for him' (55). Sarah goes through a very similar thought process at the end of the chapter. She now views her home as a kind of prison – or at least as somewhere she will never be free to leave. All those locked-in women in Victorian novels are in my mind now, in their attics and cold bedchambers, behind their veils and under their carceral domestic arrangements, entrammelled in their restrictive social sphere. In acknowledging her constraint Sarah Morley passes the torch on to the newborn son: 'At least Bryan will escape,' she thinks. The elder brother she considers to be too much like his father (60).

It is becoming clear now that the prodigal child of the title is Bryan rather than Alan. Alan will perhaps be the regulation elder brother – the new embodiment of the father, the successor, the disapprover. Bryan will be our runaway, and we will be asked to sympathise with him, I suspect.

There is a subtle but definite shift underway in chapter five. It gives an account of a Christmas day. Young Bryan focuses on the visit of Father Christmas, while his elder brother has already entered his post-Santa maturity. Significantly, young Bryan is given a toy train – an image of travel and escape, one suspects, but – and this borders on symbolism, I'm afraid – his big brother breaks it. I think I see the parable heaving into view now. As they lie in bed that night, Alan breaks the code of sibling silence and tells his brother the awful truth about Christmas. But Bryan is committed to his childish idealism – he reasserts his will to believe. The 'shift' I have alluded to is that of what was once known as the 'focaliser' – the privileged consciousness towards whose perceptions a narrative is biased, or from whose perspective, more or less, the action is seen to unfold. I suppose I owe this notion to structuralist analysis – especially in its narratological guise. Even though I am convinced that structuralism was a profoundly misconceived and philosophically indefensible project, I am not immune to the persuasiveness of such insights. It would be a shame to deny myself the use of so fitting an instrument just for the sake of theoretical purity. Anyway, call him 'focaliser' or 'privileged consciousnes' or even 'hero', we are now travelling with Bryan and the foregoing chapters may well become his prehistory.

Chapters six and seven deal with the schoolboy sexual awakening of Bryan, firstly in the self-display of a female classmate, and secondly in a friendship with Margaret – the daughter of the Spencers. Chapter seven also includes a moment of existential angst precipitated by Margaret's apparently insouciant atheism. Bryan goes to Sunday school and believes in God and the Devil, but Margaret's sense of the pointlessness of religion reminds him of his earlier need to believe in Father Christmas. There is a potent description of the nausea evoked by a world that is rich in meaningless detail, as some kind of physical illness grips the boy. That blend of the physical and the metaphysical, the melding of sensual disgust and spiritual alienation, is very well done and horribly familiar. I begin to feel the power of a kind of romanticist hermeneutics: I am entering into what Friedrich Schleiermacher thought of as a divinatory, or at least empathic, appreciation of Bryan's angst. As with structuralism, I know that such ideas are illegitimate, passé, defunct; such a moment belongs to reading, maybe, but certainly not to *a reading*. I know that I should pass over this moment silently. Please excuse me.

Chapter eight is in two parts. The first, short episode details the digging of a hole in a field as the basis for a den. It illustrates Bryan's separation, his sense of his own distinctiveness from his peers. They dig while he fashions figures from the clay spoil. He physically removes himself, taking clay from the field into the porch and continuing his modelling there. There is another of those symbolic moments when Bryan's mother comes out, accidentally steps on one of his figures, and complains about the mess he is making. I say it is 'symbolic' because I need that old fashioned term to indicate that it is suggestive of a deeper reality: it is a momentary manifestation of an underlying set of relationships. Where does this perception belong? To reading, or to *a reading*? Or is it the kind of observation that may connect one with the other? Bryan reflects that he does not belong with his family, that he cannot be the true son of his parents. Although he is not aware of what distinguishes him, the episode suggests that what alienates him from his working-class roots are artistic sensibilities that have no outlet in the context of this hand-to-mouth existence shaped by necessities. A brutal scene follows in which one of the girls is subjected to a kind of sexual assault: she is pushed into the hole and not allowed out until she removes her knickers and lifts her skirt. Bryan seems aloof – neither joining in nor assisting the girl.

The second part of the chapter builds on this burgeoning sense of alienation when Bryan returns to the Spencers' farm. He becomes aware now of the class differential between his father and Mr Spencer, and of how he seems to belong with the Spencers rather than with his father. Mr Spencer's sister – Fay Corrigan – appears, and Bryan is instantly infatuated with her. She represents an enviable urbanity and sophistication, and her presence serves to deepen his sense that he does not belong with his family. As an interpretation of the prodigal, this is an inversion of the parable in the sense that Bryan wants to escape from a poor working-class environment rather than from wealth, comfort and privilege.

Following an incident in which he helps the Corrigans to change a wheel on their car, the latter send Bryan a present of an expensive box of paints. He paints a picture of Mrs Corrigan and sends it to her, and is sub-

sequently invited to tea at their grand house. The present suggests, of
course, that the Corrigans recognise Bryan's artistic nature. The gift of the
box of paints highlights a growing tension in chapters nine and ten
between Bryan and his elder brother. If we are looking for patterns we may
be reminded of the toy train incident as Alan fiddles carelessly with the
brushes. He resents what he sees as Bryan's luck — the fact that the
Spencers treat him to cinema trips and the Corrigans buy him presents.
This, in turn, makes Bryan wonder why, given the fact that he enjoys privileges not available to his brother, he still feels 'at a disadvantage' (131).
Privilege is never enough for the prodigal because it is not uniqueness, nor
originality, nor true distinction, nor achievement. Nor is the elder
brother's pain enough. A *mutual* resentment is crucial. Without it nothing
is created. Again, these chapters have their symbolic moments: Alan
accompanies his younger brother on the bus trip to the Corrigans' house,
but Bryan leaves him at their gate as he treads the path to the front door
of the gracious home, looking back at him as a slightly ridiculous figure,
about whom there is 'an air of absurdity' (135).

. . .

I am wondering now about another meaning of 'estate' as social standing,
status, class. Is class a part of our estate? By which I mean — do we inherit
it? I have about me a degree of confused class consciousness that has led me
to find academe both highly appealing and a little too relentlessly middle
class for a boy from the south Wales valleys. I have to confess that the issue
made me uncomfortable as a child — to the extent that I was aware of it —
because we lived in a mining town, but had no material connection with
the industry. We were poor — considerably poorer than the families of most
miners — but my parents were Tories in an area that the Labour Party must
still think of as 'home'. My mother strove to prevent her children from
acquiring what she thought of as a 'valleys' accent; to be 'well-spoken' was
second only to being 'born again' in her idiosyncratic value system. This
sociopathic detachment derived, in part, from the fact that my grandparents on both sides had been tenant farmers in mid Wales, and my father's
early working life, prior to his entry into the ministry, were spent as a farm-
worker and lay preacher in Radnorshire. So the reasons for our not being
allowed to belong were not only political, but also religious; we were
Christians of a staunchly evangelical kind as well as Tories; we were saved,
called out, set apart — *aphorismenos*; we were 'in the world, but not of it.' As
such we disapproved of most things and of most people. It is easy to be a
prodigal, you might think, in such circumstances. In fact, I have found it

extremely difficult to separate myself from the already separated. I read – tendentiously, I confess – something like this into Bryan's dilemma about how to resent his brother's resentment.

. . .

Re-reading what I have written up to this point, I note that I am revising my impressions as I go. Early ideas about surveillance, time, and echoes of Hardy now seem faintly implausible. All I have by way of pattern at the moment is the relationship between the novel and the parable. It is a good thing this is not a reading.

. . .

Chapter eleven sees Bryan returning from the Corrigans to find the house empty. His brother comes in and they talk a little, Alan seeming genuinely interested in the prospects for his brother that might be the upshot of the Corrigans' interest in him. The resentment appears to be transforming itself into an impetus for Alan to make something of himself – he imagines becoming a boxer. On the other hand, Bryan's despising of his brother is undiminished. Their father comes home and collapses in a drunken stupor on the floor, and it leads to the kind of moment of negative recognition familiar from Gosse's *Father and Son*: 'Bryan felt that he had been cut off from his father for good; he could never imagine him to be again the father that he had known before' (153). At this point the echo of another text is not only strong, but it directly connects with my specific concerns. All well and good to hear echoes of Hardy, Eliot and other Victorians, but this is germane to my needs in way that those authors are not. There is, then, more than one kind of echo. Some are best ignored.

In Gosse's story it was the recognition that his father was neither omniscient nor infallible that initiated the process of escape; in Storey's novel it is a literal and metaphorical fall – the revelation of weakness, the exposure of physical and moral finitude. The prodigal must both love and despise the father; this is the lore.

. . .

In reading this chapter I notice something else: something about myself as a reader. I have subconsciously written something out. The sentence that triggered the realisation occurs in the dialogue between the two boys as they discuss the visit to the Corrigans: 'They have a servant,' Bryan observes

(151). On reading that remark, I realised that in my brief treatment of the visit to the Corrigans I had not mentioned the servant in question – Mrs Meredith. Why not? I think the logic of that oversight goes something like this: the occurrence of the servant seemed to cut across the connection between Bryan and Mrs Corrigan, which bridges a class divide. Suddenly, I recall that while reading the account of the visit I felt a certain unease about how working-class Bryan might relate to the servant who waits on him in the big house. This formed an emotional cross-current to the ambivalence I feel in both sympathising with, and – simultaneously – disapproving of, Bryan's aspiration to leave behind his working-class life. Similarly, I both resent the patronage represented by the Corrigans, and yet understand young Bryan's sense of hope that his distinction is recognised by people with the means to make a material difference to his life. I subconsciously edited the servant out because I could not locate her within the emergent structure of an already tendentious reading. She did not figure in my narrative of resentment and so she ran counter to the energies cathected in the channel of my implicit approach. Such cross-currents are a familiar feature of my reading, and they produce an anxiety that manifests itself in the processes of selection and de-selection that shape a critical response.

. . .

The break comes in chapter twelve. The Corrigans write to the Morleys asking permission to enter Bryan into a private school. It will mean Bryan residing at their house during the week, and going home on weekends. The discussion of the issue between the Morleys centres on the apparent unfairness to Alan of the arrangement. Mrs Morley argues that if a similar opportunity came along for Alan, they would not turn it down; Mr Morley simply thinks that it cannot be fair that Bryan should have an opportunity denied to Alan. Bryan says that he wants to accept the offer, and Alan – apparently unselfishly – thinks he should. Mr Morley suspects that Bryan is glad of the opportunity to leave home; Bryan denies this.

The following chapter sees Bryan moving into his room at the Corrigans, and Mrs Corrigan taking him shopping for new clothes. During their visit to town, Bryan sees his mother in her shabby clothes, and drags Mrs Corrigan down a side street to avoid a meeting. The act is an ambiguous one, of course: he is embarrassed by her shabbiness, but also thinks the meeting might embarrass her. As Bryan and Mrs Corrigan walk home, we are given a glimpse of her childhood as they pass through the poorer parts of town where she grew up. In an echo of Bryan's own sentiments, she tells him: 'I was determined to get out of it as soon as I could' (187). What precisely do they want to escape, this odd couple? Poverty? Deprivation? Narrowness of existence? The working class? Or is it something less obvious? For Bryan it seems to be an intangible something – a sense that he is better – in some indefinable way – than his family. In pondering why Mrs Corrigan has elected him for her charitable attention, he tells himself 'that Mrs Corrigan was aware of who he was' (161). This means nothing and everything. It means nothing because neither he nor the reader know who he is. Who does he think he is? we might want to ask. Yet it also means everything because it is a recognisable sentiment that is formative of the self. More than a sentiment – an assumption and a memory. Maybe it is even a condition of self-production. I suspect that every attempt to distinguish oneself, to emerge from the blurred background of the generality, is driven by the same urge, the same uninhibited flexion of the ego. In this sense, prodigality – in its guise of the urge to escape – is an orientation towards ourselves that demands we split ourselves off from what makes us: that we become other than our origins. Inasmuch as we write to be published, there is no difference here between our texts and ourselves; texts *must* be distinguished because they bear our names. We become them, they us. We are defined by what we produce, by what bears our name to the world.

Bryan starts at his new school in chapter fourteen, and is befriended by a boy called Parkinson who seems to be a bit of a loner. He takes Bryan to a seedy pub during a lunch hour. The prose is curiously impassive, and coldly observant as Bryan himself seems to be. There is little real engagement with his surroundings evident in Bryan's demeanour – with either people or places, other than Mrs Corrigan. She meets him from school and takes him to some posh tea rooms. He is intensely aware of her, of her scent, her clothes, her interaction with friends and acquaintances, even her insecurities. His contact with her is sexually charged without ever being explicitly so. This is highlighted when she holds his hand under the table in the tea room: 'Beneath his hand he could feel her skirt and, beneath her skirt, the smoothness of her stocking' (201). The subtlety of this mild eroticism is contrasted rather brutally in the following chapter when Bryan goes home and is quizzed crudely about her by his brother:

> 'You could give her a grope.' His brother paused. 'You know what
> a grope is?'
> 'No,' he said.
> 'You know what a quim is?'
> 'No.'
> His brother waited.
> 'What about jess?'

He shook his head.

'Jess,' his brother said, 'are a woman's breasts. A quim is what she has between her legs. A grope is when she lets you feel her.'

There was no connection between what his brother was telling him and what he knew of Mrs Corrigan, just as there was no connection, any longer, between his brother and himself, (205)

Mrs Corrigan has come to represent the detachment that Bryan experiences not only from his family but from the world at large. She is the embodiment of his art. She supplied him with his first box of paints and his first brushes; she was the first thing he painted; he observes her forms and colours above all else; he imagines her when she is absent. Once more, I observe with some glee, there is a close parallel between this novel and *Father and Son* in the sense that in Gosse's book the absent mother becomes identified with the art of writing; writing becomes a surrogate mother. For Bryan, Mrs Corrigan becomes a surrogate mother who is identified with his art. Perhaps this is why mothers are mostly absent from stories of the prodigal son: the story itself – or the art that draws the prodigal away from home, away, that is, from the law of the father – is the mother. If this makes her sound passive and instrumental, that may be the product of a particular ideological formation within which Storey's novel and the parable it reworks take shape. I am thinking of it in relation to desire: the way in which textual production, and artistic production more generally, are actively driven, or even birthed, by their means. As Herman Hesse put it: 'He had not to follow art, but his mother's voice'.[3]

Margaret, the atheist daughter of the Spencers, begins to emerge as a Nietzschean in chapter sixteen. Bryan visits the farm, and Margaret engages in some kind of an examination of his motives, his agenda, and his potential, but in a curiously indirect manner. Initially, it takes the form of an exchange with her mother about the pointlessness of life without God. If there is no God, then what is to stop us doing whatever we like? Mrs Spencer thinks that this kind of outlook would lead to anarchy, but Margaret opines that most people would struggle to uphold the law, while some would question what their lives were for, and transcend the limits observed by others. At this point, the significance of the discussion is made manifest:

'What do you think Bryan?' Mrs Spencer asked.

'I don't know what she means,' he said.

'Of course he understands,' Margaret said. 'It's him I'm talking about,' she added. (220)

Bryan 'wants to be someone special,' Margaret says, so the normal rules do not apply to him (221). It is clear that – despite her only appearing occasionally – Margaret is the most intelligent and perceptive figure in the novel, and she seems to understand Bryan better than he does himself. There is another exchange a little later in the chapter that illustrates the incisiveness of Margaret's mind. She asks Bryan if he is still committed to his own uniqueness:

> 'This special destiny you have, which licenses everything that happens.'
> 'I haven't given it up,' he said.
> . . . 'I have to do it my way,' Bryan said.
> 'Oh, your way,' she said. 'Well there's only the one way. I might have known you'd cover it up. Though why with me,' she added, 'I've no idea. With me especially, Bryan.'
> . . . as he mounted the bus she called, 'As for you, I'm not sure what you're really up to . . . '. (224)

Much is unspoken here, and I cannot say I know precisely what Margaret means by 'the one way', but I suspect most readers would sympathise with her sense of bafflement with regard to Bryan's agenda.

The Nietzschean image of the artist as self-transcending, self-regulating individual, untrammelled by conventional morality is furthered by the rest of the chapter which details Bryan's sculpting of a nude female figure in his school art class. I am reminded again of Herman Hesse's *Narziss and Goldmund,* although there is really little beside sculpture and echoes of Nietzsche to connect this novel with that one.

Bryan's art teacher – Miss Lightowler – is impressed and helps him to create a cast. When it is displayed in a cabinet, however, one teacher – Dr Beckerman – becomes apoplectic. He is the embodiment of the 'old school' in more senses than one: the stuffiness he represents is rather overdone, I think; he is almost a caricature: he teaches classics, is religious, a humourless disciplinarian, and dresses conservatively. Of course, the construction of the prodigal usually requires, if not quite the misrepresentation, then at least the exaggeration of the reactionary characteristics of the establishment figures that are vilified in order to distinguish the *bona fides* of the rebel, escapee, or refusenik.

Mrs Corrigan takes Bryan to the theatre, where they meet Miss Lightowler who is a set-painter there. She introduces them to an actor who charms Mrs Corrigan to the extent that she meets up with him again – much to Bryan's chagrin. Bryan is clearly jealous, and there are the first hints of a rift between them. Even before the incident with the actor, Bryan has a moment of doubt about his relationship with her. As the play begins he asks himself: 'Am I mad . . . Can't I experience anything unless, first of all, it come through her?' (237). I am thinking of Paul and the basket in which he went over the wall: the enclosure that is also transport: the confinement that brings freedom. I am thinking too of the skin trunk – the text pasted to its cramped interior, freeing the mind of the young Gosse: the confined space within which literature does its work for liberty. Mrs Corrigan, perhaps, embodies these womb-like spaces we've all come through.

Later on in chapter seventeen, Mrs Spencer dies, and the Corrigans, along with Bryan, go to the farm to see Mr Spencer and Margaret. Prior to this Mrs Corrigan has come home upset, having been with the actor. It seems likely that Mr Corrigan is aware of what is going on, but there is no real confrontation. At the farm, Mr Spencer asks Bryan to stay, and he agrees. Now it is Mrs Corrigan's turn to feel jealous. The chapter ends with a telling conversation between them in the farmyard:

> 'I don't think it was a wise thing to agree to Mr Spencer's whim. It's not as if I didn't care about what you're doing.' The tears reappeared at the corners of her eyes.
> 'What about the actor?' Bryan said.
> . . .
> 'If I've made a fool of myself,' she said, 'you don't have to rub it in . . . I don't think I could bear it if you stay here for very long.'
> 'Why not?'
> 'I need you at Chevet. You don't know how I feel at present'. (256)

The extraordinary character of the relationship is evident here. She speaks to him as though he were an adult. It occurs to me now, that I have no idea how old he is supposed to be at this point, but he is still a schoolboy. That Bryan connects his agreeing to stay at the farm with Mrs Corrigan's dalliance with the actor suggests that they both know that some kind of intense bond between them produces jealousy for each other's attention; Margaret is some kind of threat to Mrs Corrigan as the actor was to Bryan. This is a kind of mother-love, but one that is semi-sexualised by the fact that they are not actually mother and son. One can sense the Oedipal in it, but stripped of guilt.

Bryan stays at the Spencers' farm for five days and when Mrs Corrigan visits the farm, the rift between them seems to be widening. (The rift is important, of course. Nothing comes in, arrives, appears, materializes nor is realized but by way of the rift). From the farm he goes home, only to find that this too is becoming in some ways unfamiliar to him, and 'the feeling that he [doesn't] belong anywhere' deepens. While Alan and his dad are out (Alan has a boxing bout), he has a conversation with his mother that signals how far apart they are. Bryan tries to express to her his sense of purpose – or at least his sense of superiority, his desire to achieve something unique and lasting:

> 'People can't be exceptional,' his mother said, 'unless it's in their natures.'
> 'What about Alan? He's trying to be special,' Bryan said.
> 'That won't last. If he isn't beaten senseless he'll grow too old to fight. How can that be special?'
> 'If we give in before we start there doesn't seem to be any purpose in doing anything,' he said.
> 'You can choose a profession. That's what Peterson's [the public school Bryan attends] is for'. (265)

This is a neat expression of the prodigal relation: the older generation realistic, defeated or cynical (depending on your age), the younger arrogant, naïve, or idealistic (depending upon your politics). The trick, for the middle-aged prodigal, I think, is to be both at once – to ply Browning's 'dangerous edge' or 'giddy line midway': to become the cynical idealist, the naïve realist, the hopeful defeatist: to continue writing about literature after theory one has to occupy such a self-contradicting position.

A new figure appears in chapter nineteen – a butcher by the name of Stan Proctor. He turns up at Spencer's farm as a friend of the family in a scene that is fraught with unnamed tension. Margaret clearly dislikes him, and Mrs Corrigan seems irritated by him. He gives Mrs Corrigan and Bryan a lift to the station, and tells Bryan that he had courted Mrs Corrigan when they were young. He also tells Bryan that Mrs Corrigan was once in service at the house of her in-laws before marrying Harold.

Chapter twenty reveals that Proctor has become Mrs Corrigan's latest lover. At this point Bryan and the Corrigans are staying in a hotel while their house is redecorated. Serendipity, I suppose, that I, too, should be – at present – redecorating my living room, dividing my time between laptop and paintbrush. The room in which I write is out of sorts – nothing is where it should be. I have to keep shunting stuff around in order to keep furniture from wet walls, and to find space in which to paint. I have to do something similar in the temporal dimension – to fit working on this writing around the other and vice versa. I should very much have liked to move out and paid someone to do it, but I can't afford to do either. Still, the obvious analogies are instructive – the covering over of flaws that it would be too time-consuming to put right, the selection of colours according to a predetermined idea of how the finished product should look, the rearranging of objects for convenience and effect, the use of materials made available by forces beyond one's control, the vague awareness that aesthetic choices are constrained in ways that seem scarcely quantifiable.

Mrs Corrigan is rather distant, and Bryan is aware that she is seeing Proctor. One evening while she is out, Mr Corrigan takes Bryan to his club, where he gets drunk and his loosened conversation offers some insights into his own character, as well as Mrs Corrigan's, and into their strange relationship. Perhaps the most interesting effect of the chapter is to suggest that 'the prodigal child' is a title that could apply to both Mr and Mrs Corrigan as well as to Bryan. Mr says of Mrs: 'She's something of a child' (282). He adds that she is untamed. There is a degree of dramatic irony about this, since Mr Corrigan himself seems somewhat childlike as he blabs uncontrollably to his young charge. Not only so, but he also reveals his own prodigal inclinations:

> 'Have you ever had the feeling you'd like to run away?'
> 'Where to?' Bryan asked.
> 'Anywhere.'
> Bryan shook his head.
> 'I often felt the temptation when I was young. I got up one morning, bought a ticket for the first train that turned up at the station, and set off for a place I'd never heard of'. (281)

Bryan briefly appears as the anti-prodigal – rooted and uninterested in escape. In what follows, one can see why:

> 'For you,' Mr Corrigan said, 'the future is an open book, with the pages, as yet, unwritten on. For me, at your age, I knew what I would have to do, whether I cared for it or not . . . My father's son. Whereas for you,' he concluded, 'everything is different'. (281–2)

This is a rather different picture from the one drawn for Bryan by his mother, with her strong sense of social hemming-in. By comparison with Mrs Morley's stringent realism, Mr Corrigan's middle-class view misplaces the limits of Bryan's working-class position: it casts an underlying lack of prospects as a kind of enviable freedom. For Mr Corrigan, to have something to live up to is also to have something to escape from, but he seems not to notice that to inherit nothing is to be forced into flight as a matter of survival. Suddenly, I am revolted by the story of the prodigal: it is a story of privilege, of decadence, of the whining self-involvement of a secure class whose scions will have their little escapades and then settle into bourgeois complacency – the system unchallenged by a trivial flirtation with social dehiscence. But the very revulsion that turns one away from an order or from a regime is itself a prodigal resentment. This parable has all the resilience of Hegelian dialectic: however hard you resist it, it reclaims you in the end. Escape is return.

It also emerges in this chapter that the Corrigans' patronage of Bryan is closely related to the problems of their marriage. When Bryan and the mildly inebriated Mr Corrigan return to the hotel, Mrs Corrigan is there, and is upset. The ensuing exchange between husband and wife – in front of Bryan – is revealing:

> 'Bryan should have been enough if you'd only controlled your appetite for creating a sensation with other men.'
> 'How can Bryan satisfy everything, Harold?'
> 'He satisfies enough . . . You can send him back.'
> 'Where?'
> 'To Stainforth.'
> 'I can't send him back. He can't go back,' Mrs Corrigan added.
>
> (285)

This chilling dialogue reveals not only the extent to which Bryan has been deluded by his dreams of true 'recognition' in the attentions of Mrs Corrigan, but also the extent to which the bourgeois values of Mr Corrigan objectify Bryan as a counter, or token, in the marriage-game of his social superiors. Mrs Corrigan's revulsion at the idea of 'sending him back' is the product of her own class sensibility: to admit the possibility that Bryan might go back would be to acknowledge that she herself is vulnerable, that the road back to poverty is still open.

The long twenty-first chapter sees Mr Corrigan fall ill and recover, and Mrs Corrigan, Bryan and Margaret go away for a holiday at some lakeside hotel. The relationship between Bryan and Mrs Corrigan continues to mystify, while that between Bryan and Margaret continues to tease. Mrs Corrigan pushes him away, and tries to persuade him to spend more time with Margaret. There is an air of mystery in her disposition; her motives so far have never been entirely clear. Meanwhile Bryan begins to see that Margaret is actually very like her aunt in some ways, but is perhaps less self-regarding. Margaret points out to Bryan that he imagines Mrs Corrigan to be 'motiveless', whilst Margaret sees that she is actually driven by motives that are mainly selfish, or, at least, are never quite selfless. It is obvious now that Mrs Corrigan is as obsessed with Bryan as he is with her, but she feels profoundly guilty about absorbing his attention and keeping him from the rest of the world. She has conceived of the holiday as a way of bringing Bryan and Margaret together in order to wean herself from him, and him from her. When she makes clear to Bryan that their relationship cannot continue, he swims out into the lake in what is possibly a suicide attempt. He survives and Mrs Corrigan tells him that he should forget what she said. The chapter ends with them swimming together – possibly naked. Symbolically, if not physically, this is the consummation of their relationship – a kind of mutual baptism. After this point, we see them together only in an air-raid shelter – she looking older and haggard, he seeming more like a dutiful son than an illicit paramour. I am reminded of Rider Haggard's *She*, and the joint bathing in the flame of eternal youth, after which Ayesha shrivels and dies. This is the phallocentric myth retold: the mystery over, the woman ceases to appeal or to matter. She is literally consumed by the male experience; she vanishes like the mother in a parable. By now Mr Corrigan is dead.

The novel closes by taking Bryan back to his home at the time of the coronation when a party is in full swing – obviously: the pattern of the parable must be observed. Cleverly, Bryan is made to meet up with his father, and to recognise something of his true character, before this return. Remember that in the parable 'when he was yet a great way off, his father saw him, and had compassion, and ran, and fell on his neck, and kissed him' (Luke 15: 20). Bryan's meeting with his father takes place in the penultimate chapter (twenty-three) a way off from home – at Feltham – where the Spencers' have their farm. In a pub, the father recognises the son's achievement, and the son recognises the father's dogged devotion to his family. It is appropriate that the meeting should be at Feltham, because it was here that Bryan met Mrs Corrigan, and it was here that he registered his greatest distance from his father – his father the employee out in the fields, while he was a guest in the house.

By the time of the coronation, Bryan is a sculptor enjoying a burgeoning success. He recognises now that the home from which he fled was actually the 'heart from which the blood is pumped, expanding . . . out to the world' (319). In a gesture that evokes the harmonious denouement of comic convention, people are dancing – his parents among them. Margaret is there too, looking like Mrs Corrigan reborn. It is moving, life-affirming and positive. But somehow it manages to turn me inside out. I have actively despised the patrons and the class privilege they represent, but now I feel that Mrs Corrigan is heedlessly and ungratefully dispatched to the prehistory of Bryan's success. I do not believe in the rebirth. To read the parable as a story of redemption – even if redemption is understood as nothing but a kind of self-actualisation – is, as we know, always to leave someone outside.

. . .

I make this jointure: the reading that follows and does not follow the text it names as its source.

. . .

This reading, appropriating the property of another, becomes my estate.

. . .

The meaning of 'estate', the story goes, has changed and can change again.

Parables of the Republic

The Prodigal Sign

I owe my title, 'The Prodigal Sign', to the poet and critic Tiffany Atkinson. The story takes place in the coffee bar of the Aberystwyth Arts Centre. Gathered around a table one sunny morning was a group of colleagues from the Department of English at the University of Wales, Aberystwyth, discussing informally their respective current research projects in the light of the looming RAE (an exercise a bit like the census declared by Caesar Augustus, but involving journal articles, books and other measurable outputs demanded of the modern academic, and with fewer journeys undertaken by pregnant women on donkeys). The atmosphere, as usual at such times, was characterised by a kind of gallows humour that involves the ritual self-deprecation of one's professional performance: you tell me how badly your research is going, and I'll tell you how much better it is than mine.

I mentioned, in this context, that I wanted to write about parables, in particular the one that tells of the prodigal son. I have in mind, I said, a half-baked theory – more accurately a conceit – that literary critics are all like the prodigal son in that we are habitual runaways – forever escaping, or seeking to escape, the jurisdiction of our forebears, of the academy, of the measurement of our research output, of teaching duties etc., always on the lookout for something new and distinctive to say about the same old texts, or for pristine new texts that no-one else knows about, or that have at least escaped the professional attention of our peers. Like the prodigal son, we live on our inheritance while trying to escape from our own disciplinary history. But we always, in some way, go back to what has been done before. I added that I did not, as yet, have a title for the projected book. There followed a round of jokey and punning suggestions, none of which, I am sorry to say, I can remember, except for Tiffany's – 'The Prodigal Sign'. I remember that one because it made us laugh, and because it was a joke that has shaped the entire project.

The Wandering Critic

There was a literary critic who was not a scholar. He would have liked to have been a scholar, but he was not one. He lacked the energy, the stamina, the monomania to invest all of his time in the manifold details of biographies, letters, journals, diaries, shopping lists, notes scribbled in the margins of books, reported *bon mots*, quips, and all the other scrapings of ink and graphite that together might constitute the complete works of an historic individual upon whom he might pronounce himself an authority. No-one whose work he had read seemed to him to be worth a lifetime's effort. Nor did he have the inclination to immerse himself in the fine workings of history in such a way that he could be considered an expert in any literary era. He found history too detailed, too contrary, too messy for his compulsively tidying mind. He was, he claimed, unable to recognise what constitutes history, to draw definitive (or even provisional) lines around any collection of signs, traces, discourses, monuments, texts, events, dates, lives etc, and unwilling, so he affirmed, to bully them into a period. He had a tendency to wander wantonly from topic to topic, to maunder from author to author, and although he endeavoured to focus his attention on 'Victorian' (he would insist on the quotation marks) literature, he dallied with Romanticism, with myth, with the Bible, with Bob Dylan, with philosophy and theology, and with the writing of poems and novels. He found this kind of dalliance infinitely preferable to trolling around libraries in search of archives, holdings, collections, manuscripts and the tiresome paraphernalia of good scholarship. These characteristics are not very promising in a literary critic who aspires to academic title. Unless the prodigal truly is the sign of his profession.

The Radio Show

What shall we say criticism is like? To what shall we compare it? Criticism is like a gameshow – or panel game – on BBC Radio 4. Or, at least, it is like one game played under the chairmanship of the late Humphrey Lyttleton in some episodes of 'I'm Sorry I Haven't a Clue' – the game called 'Mornington Crescent'. The game involves each player in turn naming a station on the underground, a road or a street in London. The first person to say 'Mornington Crescent' wins. Each time it is played, a set of ever-changing, fictional rules seems to be in place, and each variant of the game has its own distinctive designation and set of abstruse sub-rules. Because the pretend 'rules' are arcane, variable, and complicated, and because the chairman is extremely capricious, what counts as a good move according to one week's imaginary protocols, might prove disastrous in the next game. The audience willingly and gleefully plays along with the charade, applauding 'clever' or 'audacious' plays, and pretending to know what's going on. Whether or not this bears any comparison with the way literary criticism works depends upon one's interpretation of Smallham's 'Displacement Protocol' (1987).

Note

Smallham's 'Displacement Protocol' is based upon the Freudian theory of dream interpretation according to which the work of the dream is to disguise the familiar by shifting emphasis from what is important in the latent dream onto less important aspects of the manifest content. Smallham's contention is that the recognition or diagnosis of this kind of displacement is itself a displacement that shifts focus away from the analyst's desire to exert mastery over the analysand by claiming to know something about them that they are unable to see for themselves. Smallham argues that literary criticism is a second-order displacement of just this kind: the critic focuses on the text's latent content, on its unsaid, or on what it represents obscurely, in order to demonstrate a mastery over literary discourse, over the author, the student, and the non-professional reader. She refers to this critical move as a 'protocol' since it amounts to a group procedure or formality definitive of the discipline. (Hermione Smallham, *The Displacement Protocol in Critical Discourse*, Cardiff: Edward James, 1987, 109–26)

The Conference

A certain critic went to a conference in a far country, for she had not attended one for nearly three years. She read (to a very small group of people who thought they saw in her work reflections – albeit faint ones – of their own interests), a paper entitled 'Disciple and Discipline'. It was about the construction of an academic discourse in terms of the models of discipleship derived from religion and philosophy. There was little time for questions from the floor at the end of her twenty-minute slot, since the paper on Margery Kempe's use of the letter 'h' had overrun by ten minutes. During the break that followed the session, over coffee and biscuits, she was approached by an eager young scholar, keen to engage her in discussion of her theoretical perspective. He had read her book, he said.

'I have no theoretical perspective,' she said, thinking of how her methodology borrowed protocols, strategies and models of the reading process, willy-nilly, from a range of diverse and divergent theoretical perspectives (from Agamben to Žižek) with prodigal inconstancy.

'Ah,' said her wise young interlocutor, 'we *all* have a theoretical perspective that we deploy consciously or unconsciously. There is no theory-neutral position from which to approach the text.'

She thought, momentarily, about clarifying her position, about putting straight his evident misapprehension of her intended meaning, but, with something like a sigh, she just smiled, glanced at his lapel badge and said:

'So, Andy, tell me about *your* work.'

She can remember nothing of what he said about his own research, not even what his field of expertise was, but she can recall his face, his name, and his zealous orthodoxy.

The Visiting Lecturer

There was a professor of English Literature with many books to his name, who was head of his department at Oxbow University. On a certain day there came to his door a visiting lecturer who politely interested herself in her host's academic output. She greatly admired, she said, his *Postmodernism for Non-traditional Entrants,* as a useful introductory text (but she did not mention the number of photocopies she had taken for her first-year 'Trying Out Theories' seminar, of Chapter Three: 'Nature, Nurture, Nietzsche'). What was he currently working on, she inquired. The professor smiled coyly:

> 'Oh, I'm doing a book on fiction sold in hypermarkets, for Blackleg.'
> 'Sounds fascinating,' she lied.
> 'It isn't,' he admitted. 'I was asked to write it, and . . . well, you know . . . RAE and all that. I sometimes wonder what it's all for, but without the books what I am is just a teacher.'

The visitor, thinking about her sister who taught History in a comprehensive school in Pontypridd, nearly asked him what was so bad about being a teacher, but thinking it might sound a little rude, she bit her tongue. She also knew, deep down, that it would be disingenuous of her to ask.

The Healing of the Man with Tachycardia

In a far country, a lecturer in English Literature at a new university became ill. His heart raced even when he rested. He lost the ability to relax, and his chest hurt most of the time. He went to see a doctor who sent him to the local hospital for a series of tests. They took his blood pressure, sampled his blood and his urine and they wired him up to an ECG. When all the results were in his doctor sent for him, and said to him:

'All the tests are done, and the results are in. Everything is normal. You look to me like a worried man. Perhaps you need to change your lifestyle.'

So the lecturer left his job at the university, and went and found work in a supermarket, stacking shelves. He found that, for the first time in ten years, he was able to relax when he came home at night.

A year later, unable to pay his mortgage on the wages of a supermarket employee, he returned to the academic life and began work on a book about running away and returning.

Notes

Introduction

1 Virginia Woolf, *The Diary of Virginia Woolf*, ed. Anne Oliver and Andrew McNeillie, 5 vols. (London: Hogarth Press, 1977–84), iii, p. 131.
2 Luce Irigaray, *The Irigaray Reader*, ed. Margaret Whitford (Oxford: Blackwell, 1991), p. 36.
3 Sandra. M. Gilbert & Susan Gubar, *The Madwoman in the Attic: The Woman Writer and the Nineteenth-Century Literary Imagination* (New Haven and London: Yale University Press, 1984), p. 6.
4 Ibid., p. 16.
5 W. Jackson Bate, *The Burden of the Past and the English Poet* (London: Chatto and Windus, 1971).
6 Frank Kermode, *The Genesis of Secrecy: On the Interpretation of Narrative* (Cambridge, Mass.: Harvard University Press, 1979), p. 4.
7 Derek Attridge & Jane Elliott, 'Putting Practice in the Theory,' in *The Times Higher Educational Supplement*, January 5, 2007, p. 16.
8 Ernst Bloch, *The Principle of Hope*, trans. Neville Plaice, Stephen Plaice and Paul Knight, 3 vols. (Oxford: Blackwell, 1986), iii, p. 1376.
9 Jill Robbins, *Prodigal Son / Elder Brother: Interpretation and Alterity in Augustine, Petrarch, Kafka, Levinas* (Chicago and London: University of Chicago Press, 1991), p. 10.
10 Ibid., p. 39.
11 Ibid., p. 38.

Parable and Criticism: The Prodigal Son

1 Johann Georg Hamann, 'A Clover-Leaf of Hellenistic Letters', in Ronald Gregor Smith, *J.G. Hamann, 1730–1788: A Study in Christian Experience with Selections from his Writings* (London: Collins, 1960), pp. 186–8, 187.
2 On this critical division, see John W. Sider, 'Rediscovering the Parables: The Logic of the Jeremias Tradition,' in *Journal of Biblical Literature* 102, 1 (1983), pp. 61–83.
3 For a digest of these approaches, see David P. Parris, 'Imitating the Parables: Allegory, Narrative and the Role of Mimesis,' in *Journal for the Study of the New Testament* 25, 1 (2002), pp. 33–53.
4 C.F. Evans, *Parable and Dogma* (London: Athlone Press, 1977), p. 5.
5 John Drury, 'Origins of Mark's Parables,' in Michael Wadsworth (ed.), *Ways of Reading the Bible* (Brighton: Harvester Press, 1981), pp. 171–89, 183.
6 Gerald L. Bruns, 'Midrash and Allegory: The Beginnings of Scriptural

Interpretation,' in Robert Alter and Frank Kermode (eds.), *The Literary Guide to the Bible* (London: Collins, 1987), pp. 625–46, 627.

7   David P. Parris, 'Imitating the Parables: Allegory, Narrative and the Role of Mimesis,' in *Journal for the Study of the New Testament* 25, 1 (2002), pp. 33–53.

8   Ibid. p. 53.

9   Bernard Harrison, 'Parable and Transcendence,' in Michael Wadsworth (ed.), *Ways of Reading the Bible*, pp. 190–212, 190.

10 John Drury, 'Luke,' in Robert Alter and Frank Kermode (eds.), *The Literary Guide to the Bible*, pp. 418–39, 427–8.

11 Bernard Harrison, 'Parable and Transcendence,' pp. 191–2.

12 Ibid., p. 196.

13 Ibid., p. 202.

14 Ibid., pp. 202–3.

15 Ibid., p. 203.

16 Giorgio Agamben, *The Time That Remains: A Commentary on the Letter to the Romans*, trans. Patricia Dailey (Stanford, Calif.: Stanford University Press, 2005), p. 42.

17 C. H. Dodd, *The Parables of the Kingdom* (Glasgow: Collins, 1961), p. 15.

18 Slavoj Žižek, 'St Paul; Or, The Christian Uncoupling,' in *The European English Messenger*, VIII, 2 (1999), pp. 45–9, 45.

19 Giorgio Agamben, *The Time That Remains*, p. 138.

20 Frank Kermode, *The Genesis of Secrecy: On the Interpretation of Narrative* (Cambridge, Mass.: Harvard University Press, 1979), p. 7.

21 C. H. Dodd, op. cit., p. 15.

22 Slavoj Žižek, op. cit., p. 45.

23 C. H. Dodd, *The Parables of the Kingdom*, p. 20.

24 Frank Kermode, *The Genesis of Secrecy*, p. 15.

25 Ibid., p. 5.

26 Jill Robbins, *Prodigal Son / Elder Brother: Interpretation and Alterity in Augustine, Petrarch, Kafka, Levinas* (Chicago and London: University of Chicago Press, 1991), p. 72.

The Dwarf

1   Walter Benjamin, *Illuminations* (London: Fontana, 1973), p. 255.

Keywords: The Prodigal Daughter

1   Valentine Cunningham, *In the Reading Gaol: Postmodernity, Texts and History* (Cambridge Mass. and Oxford: Blackwell, 1994). Page numbers are given in the text from here on.

2   Jacques Derrida, *Writing and Difference*, trans. Alan Bass (London: Routledge and Kegan Paul, 1978), pp. 278–93.

3   Frank Kermode, *The Genesis of Secrecy: On the Interpretation of Narrative* (Cambridge, Mass.: Harvard University Press, 1979), p. 20.

4   Helen Keller, *The Story of My Life* (London: Hodder and Stoughton, 1949). Page numbers are given in the text from here on.

5   Paul Ricoeur, *Time and Narrative*, Vol. 3, trans. Kathleen Blamey and David Pellauer (Chicago and London: University of Chicago Press, 1988), pp. 247–9. See also Paul Ricoeur, 'Narrative Identity,' trans. David Wood, in David Wood (ed.), *On Paul Ricoeur: Narrative and Interpretation* (London: Routledge, 1991, pp. 188–99). In the latter essay Ricoeur writes: 'Narrative mediation underlines this remarkable characteristic of self-knowledge – that it is self-interpretation' (p. 198). It is just this act of self-interpretation that allows Keller to reaffirm her self in the aftermath of the the an agnostic crisis.

6   Jacques Derrida, *Writing and Difference*, p. 279. Play, here, has to do with the space or scope for movement within a structure. Elements within a structure only have such freedom if the structure is somehow loosened. If the structurality of structure is constructed around the linguistic sign (as in structuralism), then the deconstruction of the sign is also the loosening up of the structure – a destabilising of its centre or organising principle that enables play.

7   Robert Browning, 'Bishop Blougram's Apology,' in Ian Jack (ed.), *Browning: Poetical Works 1833–1864* (Oxford: Oxford University Press, 1970), pp. 645–72.

The Broken Doll

1   Martin Heidegger, 'The Way to Language', trans. David Farrell Krell, in David Farrell Krell (ed.), *Martin Heidegger: Basic Writings* (London: Routledge, 1993), pp. 397–426, 407–8.

2   Julia Kristeva, *Revolution in Poetic Language*, trans Margaret Waller, in Kelly Oliver (ed.), *The Portable Kristeva* (New York: Columbia University Press, 1997), pp. 27–92, 48.

3   Andrew Gibson, *Postmodernity, Ethics and the Novel: From Leavis to Levinas* (London and New York: Routledge, 1999), p. 85.

4   Paul Ricoeur, 'The Problem of Double Meaning as Hermeneutic Problem and as Semantic Problem', trans. Kathleen McLaughlin, in Don Ihde (ed.), *The Conflict of Interpretations: Essays in Hermeneutics* (Evanston: Northwestern University Press, 1974), pp. 62–78, 63.

5   Leonard Cohen, 'Anthem', from the album *The Future* (Columbia, 1992).

6   Johann Georg Hamann, 'Fragments,' in Ronald Gregor Smith, *J.G. Hamann, 1730–1788: A Study in Christian Experience with Selections from his Writings* (London: Collins, 1960), pp. 160–73, 161.

7   Daniel Boyarin, *Intertextuality and the Reading of Midrash* (Bloomington: Indiana University Press, 1990), p. 12.

8   Julia Kristeva, *Strangers to Ourselves*, trans Leon Roudiez, in Kelly Oliver (ed.), *The Portable Kristeva*, pp. 264–94, 274.

9   Jacques Derrida, *The Gift of Death*, trans. David Willis (Chicago and London: The University of Chicago Press, 1995), p. 92.

10   George Herbert, 'The Windows'.

The Strange Face of Dr Jekyll and Mr Hyde

1   *The Acts of Paul and Thecla*, in *The Ante-Nicene Fathers VIII*. Edinburgh: T&T Clark; Grand Rapids, Michigan: Wm B. Eerdmans, 1995, pp. 487–92, 487.

2   Robert Louis Stevenson, *Virginibus Puerisque & Other Papers* (Harmondsworth: Penguin, 1946), p. 57.

3   Philip Sellew, 'Interior Monologue as a Narrative Device in the Parables of Luke,' in *Journal of Biblical Literature*, vol. 111, no. 2 (1992), pp. 239–53, 239–40.

4   Richard Rorty, *Philosophy and the Mirror of Nature* (Princeton NJ: Princeton UP, 1980).

5   René Descartes, *Philosophical Writings*, eds E. Anscombe & P.T. Geach (London: Thomas Nelson & The Open University Press, 1970), p. 14.

6   Immanual Kant, *Critique of Pure Reason*, trans. N. K. Smith (Basingstoke & London: Macmillan, 1929), p. 10.

7   Friedrich Nietzsche, *Selections*, ed. Richard Schact (Englewood Cliffs, NJ: Prentice-Hall, 1993), p. 171.

8   Karl Marx, *The German Ideology*, in Eugene Kamenka (ed.), *The Portable Karl Marx* (Harmondsworth: Penguin, 1983), pp. 162–195, 169.

9   Sigmund Freud, *The Ego and the Id* (Harmondsworth: Penguin 1975); Jacques Lacan, *The Works of Jacques Lacan*, eds. B. Benvenuto & R. Kennedy (London: Free Association Books, 1986); Luce Irigaray, *Speculum of the Other Woman*, trans. Gillian C. Gill (Ithaca and London: Cornell UP, 1985).

10   William James, *The Varieties of Religious Experience: A Study in Human Nature* (Harmondsworth: Penguin, 1986), p. 189.

11   Robert Louis Stevenson, *Virginibus Puerisque & Other Papers*, p. 55.

12   Ibid., p. 57.

13   Jill Robbins, *Prodigal Son / Elder Brother: Interpretation and Alterity in Augustine, Petrarch, Kafka, Levinas* (Chicago and London: University of Chicago Press, 1991), p. 24.

14   Augustine, *Confessions*, trans. J. G. Pilkington (Edinburgh: T&T Clark, 1876), VIII, v.

15   John Kelman, *The Faith of Robert Louis Stevenson* (Edinburgh & London: Oliphant, Anderson and Ferrier, 1912), pp. 220–1.

16   J. P. Hennessy, *Robert Louis Stevenson* (London: Jonathan Cape, 1974), pp. 55–6.

17   Ibid., p. 180.

18   Edwin M. Eigner, *Robert Louis Stevenson and Romantic Tradition* (Princeton, NJ: Princeton UP, 1966), p. 148.

19   Robert Louis Stevenson, 'The Strange Case of Dr Jekyll and Mr Hyde,' in *Dr Jekyll and Mr Hyde and Other Stories* (London: Penguin, 1979), p. 83. From here on, page references for this edition are given in the text.

20   *The Acts of Paul and Thecla*, p. 487.

21   R. L. Cross, *The Early Christian Fathers* (London: Duckworth, 1960), p. 80.

Reason's Disciple: After Master Derrida

1   Jorge Luis Borges, *Labyrinths* (Harmondsworth: Penguin, 1970), pp. 125–30.
2   Walter Kaufmann (ed.), *The Portable Nietzsche* (Harmondsworth: Penguin, 1976), p. 58.
3   Paul Ricoeur, 'Interpretative Narrative,' trans. D. Pellauer, in Regina Schwartz (ed.), *The Book and the Text: The Bible and Literary Theory* (Oxford: Basil Blackwell, 1990), pp. 237–57, 244.
4   Jacques Derrida, *Of Grammatology*, trans. G. C. Spivak (Baltimore & London: Johns Hopkins University Press.1976), pp. 65–73.
5   Jacques Derrida, 'Plato's Pharmacy,' in *Dissemination*, trans. B Johnson (London: Athlone, 1981), pp. 61–171.
6   René Descartes, *Philosophical Writings*, ed. and trans. E. Anscombe & P. T. Geach (London: Thomas Nelson & The Open University Press, 1970), p. 14.
7   Ibid, p. 15.
8   Friedrich Nietzsche, *Selections*, ed. Richard Schact (Englewood Cliffs, NJ: Prentice-Hall, 1993), p. 171.
9   Immanuel Kant, *Critique of Pure Reason*, trans. N. K. Smith (Basingstoke & London: Macmillan, 1929), p. 10.
10   Ibid., p. 10.
11   Jacques Derrida, *Of Grammatology*, p. 66.
12   Augustine, *Confessions*, trans. J. G. Pilkington (Edinburgh: T&T Clark, 1876), VIII, v.
13   Jill Robbins, *Prodigal Son / Elder Brother: Interpretation and Alterity in Augustine, Petrarch, Kafka, Levinas* (Chicago and London: University of Chicago Press, 1991), p. 59. My emphasis.
14   Slavoj Žižek, 'Revaluations: St Paul; Or, The Christian Uncoupling,' in *The European English Messenger*, VIII / 2 (1999), pp. 45–9, 46.
15   Ibid., p. 48.

Father Away in the Forest of Books

1   John Russell Brown, *Shakespeare: The Tragedies* (Houndmills: Palgrave, 2001), p. 231.
2   Terry Eagleton, *William Shakespeare* (Oxford: Blackwell, 1986), p. x.
3   Michael Mangan, *A Preface to Shakespeare's Comedies 1594–1603* (London: Longman, 1996), p. 202.
4   Paul Yachnin, 'Shakespeare's Problem Plays and the Drama of His Time: *Troilus and Cressida, All's Well That Ends Well, Measure for Measure*,' in Richard Dutton and Jean Howard (eds.), *A Companion to Shakespeare's Works Volume IV: The Poems, Problem Comedies, Late Plays* (Oxford: Blackwell, 2003), pp. 46–68, 59.
5   Louis Montrose, ' "The Place of a Brother" in *As You Like It*: Social Process and Comic Form,' in Ivo Kamps (ed.), *Materialist Shakespeare: A History* (London: Verso, 1995), pp. 39–70, 41.

6   Ivo Kamps, 'Introduction,' in *Materialist Shakespeare*, p. 9.

7   Louis Montrose, '"The Place of a Brother" in *As You Like It*,' p. 59.

8   Regenia Gagnier, 'Money, the Economy, and Social Class,' in Patrick Brantlinger & William B. Thesing (eds.), *A Companion to the Victorian Novel* (Oxford: Blackwell, 2002), pp. 48–66, 60. Gagnier uses this phrase in discussing *Great Expectations*.

9   Louis Montrose, '"The Place of a Brother" in *As You Like It*,' p. 52.

10 Ibid., p. 49.

11 I am indebted to Jonathan Taylor's admirably clear and concise account of the master–slave dialectic, in *Mastery and Slavery in Victorian Writing* (Basingstoke: Palgrave Macmillan, 2003).

Splitting the Aphorism

1   Giorgio Agamben, *The Time That Remains: A Commentary on the Letter to the Romans*, trans. Patricia Dailey (Stanford, Calif.: Stanford University Press, 2005), pp. 45–6.

2   Giorgio Agamben, *The Time That Remains*, p. 46.

3   Franz Kafka, *Description of a Struggle and Other Stories*, trans. Willa and Edwin Muir, Malcolm Pasley, Tania and James Stern (Harmondsworth: Penguin, 1979), p. 152.

4   Giorgio Agamben, *The Time That Remains*, p. 45.

5   Ibid., p. 51.

6   Ibid., p. 55.

Skin Trunk: Literature and Resistance in *Father and Son*

1   Robert Browning, 'Bishop Blougram's Apology,' in Ian Jack (ed.), *Browning: Poetical Works 1833–1864* (Oxford: Oxford University Press, 1970), pp. 645–72.

2   Peter Allen, 'Sir Edmund Gosse and His Modern Readers: The Continued Appeal of *Father and Son*,' in *ELH*, 55, 2 (1988), pp. 487–503, 488.

3   Jacques Derrida, *Of Grammatology*, trans. G.C. Spivak (Baltimore & London: Johns Hopkins University Press, 1976), p. 39.

4   Edmund Gosse, *Father and Son* (Harmondsworth: Penguin, 1970), p. 177. References to this edition are given in the text from here on.

5   Ann Thwaite, *Edmund Gosse: A Literary Landscape, 1849–1928* (London: Secker & Warburg, 1984), p. 493.

6   Peter Allen, 'Sir Edmund Gosse and His Modern Readers,' p. 491.

7   Robert Louis Stevenson, 'The Strange Case of Dr Jekyll and Mr Hyde,' in *Dr Jekyll and Mr Hyde and Other Stories* (London: Penguin, 1979), p. 61.

8   Ann Thwaite, *Edmund Gosse*, p. 348.

9   Peter Allen, 'Sir Edmund Gosse and His Modern Readers,' p. 494.

10 Edmund Gosse, 'The Prodigal,' from *In Russet and Silver* (London: William Heinemann, 1894), pp. 48–9.

11 J. D. Woolf, *Sir Edmund Gosse* (New York: Twayne Publishers, Inc., 1972), pp. 152–3.

12 Ann Thwaite, *Edmund Gosse*, p. 11.
13 Ibid., p. 303.
14 Lee Krenis, 'Authority and Rebellion in Victorian Autobiography,' in *The Journal of British Studies*, 18, 1 (1978), pp. 107–30, 108.
15 Ibid., p. 109.
16 Ibid., p. 119.
17 Ibid., p. 122.
18 Ann Thwaite, *Edmund Gosse*, p. 314.
19 Ibid., p. 339.
20 Harold Orel, *Victorian Literary Critics: George Henry Lewes, Walter Bagehot, Richard Holt Hutton, Leslie Stephen, Andrew Lang, George Saintsbury and Edmund Gosse* (London: Macmillan, 1984), p. 178.
21 Ibid., p. 179.
22 Ann Thwaite, *Edmund Gosse*, p. 479.
23 Ibid., p. 359.
24 Frederic R. Ross, 'Philip Gosse's *Omphalos*, Edmund Gosse's *Father and Son*, and Darwin's Theory of Natural Selection,' in *Isis*, 68, 1 (1977), pp. 85–96, 86.
25 Harold Orel, *Victorian Literary Critics*, p. 178.
26 Peter Allen, 'Sir Edmund Gosse and His Modern Readers,' p. 488.
27 Ann Thwaite, *Edmund Gosse*, p. 3.
28 Frederic R. Ross, 'Philip Gosse's *Omphalos*, Edmund Gosse's *Father and Son*, and Darwin's Theory of Natural Selection,' pp. 86, 93, 95.
29 See Frederic R. Ross, 'Philip Gosse's *Omphalos*, Edmund Gosse's *Father and Son*, and Darwin's Theory of Natural Selection,' p. 95, n.32.
30 Ann Thwaite, *Edmund Gosse*, p. 233.
31 Ibid., p. 234.

The Estate

1 David Storey, *A Prodigal Child* (London: Jonathan Cape, 1982). Page numbers are given in the text.
2 For a detailed reading of the treatment of time in *Far From the Madding Crowd*, see Kevin Mills, *Approaching Apocalypse: Unveiling Revelation in Victorian Writing* (Lewisburg: Bucknell University Press, 2007), pp. 134–43.
3 Herman Hesse, *Narziss and Goldmund*, trans. Geoffrey Dunlop (Harmondsworth: Penguin, 1971), p. 179.

Index